BLESSING

OVERTURES TO BIBLICAL THEOLOGY

A series of studies in biblical theology designed
to explore fresh dimensions of research and to
suggest ways in which the biblical heritage may
address contemporary culture

Editors

WALTER BRUEGGEMANN, Dean of Academic Affairs
and Professor of Old Testament at Eden Theological Seminary

JOHN R. DONAHUE, S.J., Associate Professor of
New Testament at Vanderbilt Divinity School

In the Bible and the Life of the Church

BLESSING

By
CLAUS WESTERMANN

Translated by
KEITH CRIM

F **FORTRESS PRESS**   Philadelphia

Translated by Keith Crim from the German *Der Segen in der Bibel und im Handeln der Kirche* © 1968 Chr. Kaiser Verlag, München.

Biblical quotations from the Revised Standard Version of the Bible, copyrighted 1946, 1952, © 1971, 1973 by the Division of Christian Education of the National Council of the Churches of Christ in the U.S.A., are used by permission.

Library of Congress Cataloging in Publication Data

Westermann, Claus.
    Blessing in the Bible and the life of the church.

    Translation of Der Segen in der Bibel und im Handeln der Kirche.
    Bibliography: p.
    Includes indexes.
    1. Blessing and cursing in the Bible. I. Title.
BS680.B5W413   234   78-54564
ISBN 0-8006-1529-8

7127E78   Printed in the United States of America   1–1529

Contents

Series Foreword

Biblical theology has been a significant part of modern study of the Jewish and Christian Scriptures. Prior to the ascendancy of historical criticism of the Bible in the nineteenth century, biblical theology was subordinated to the dogmatic concerns of the churches, and the Bible too often provided a storehouse of rigid proof texts. When biblical theology was cut loose from its moorings to dogmatic theology to become an enterprise seeking its own methods and categories, attention was directed to what the Bible itself had to say. A dogmatic concern was replaced by an historical one so that biblical theology was understood as an investigation of what was believed by different communities in different situations. By the end of the nineteenth century biblical theology was virtually equated with the history of the religion of the authors who produced biblical documents or of the communities which used them.

While these earlier perspectives have become more refined and sophisticated, they still describe the parameters of what is done in the name of biblical theology—moving somewhere between the normative statements of dogmatic theology and the descriptive concerns of the history of religions. Th. Vriezen, in his *An Outline of Old Testament Theology* (Dutch, 1949; ET, 1958), sought to combine these concerns by devoting the first half of his book to historical considerations and the second half to theological themes. But even that effort did not break out of the stalemate of categories. In more recent times Old Testament theology has been dominated by two paradigmatic works. In his *Theology of the Old Testament* (German, 1933–39; ET,

1967) W. Eichrodt has provided a comprehensive statement around fixed categories which reflect classical dogmatic interests, although the centrality of covenant in his work reflects the Bible's own categories. By contrast, G. von Rad in his *Old Testament Theology* (German, 1960; ET, 1965) has presented a study of theological traditions with a primary concern for the historical dynamism of the traditions. In the case of New Testament theology, historical and theological concerns are rather roughly juxtaposed in the work of A. Richardson, *An Introduction to the Theology of the New Testament.* As in the case of the Old Testament there are two major options or presentations which dominate in New Testament studies. The history-of-religion school has left its mark on the magisterial work of R. Bultmann, who proceeds from an explanation of the expressions of faith of the earliest communities and their theologians to a statement of how their understanding of existence under faith speaks to us today. The works of O. Cullmann and W. G. Kümmel are clear New Testament statements of *Heilsgeschichte* under the aegis of the tension between promise and fulfillment—categories reminiscent of von Rad.

As recently as 1962 K. Stendahl again underscored the tension between historical description and normative meaning by assigning to the biblical theologian the task of describing what the Bible *meant,* not what it *means* or *how* it can have meaning. However, this objectivity of historical description is too often found to be a mirror of the observer's hidden preunderstanding, and the adequacy of historical description is contingent on one generation's discoveries and postulates. Also, the yearning and expectation of believers and would-be believers will not let biblical theology rest with the descriptive task alone. The growing strength of Evangelical Protestantism and the expanding phenomenon of charismatic Catholicism are but vocal reminders that people seek in the Bible a source of alternative value systems. By its own character and by the place it occupies in our culture the Bible will not rest easy as merely an historical artifact.

Thus it seems a fitting time to make "overtures" concerning biblical theology. It is not a time for massive tomes which claim too much. It appears not even to be a time for firm conclusions which are too comprehensive. It is a time for pursuit of fresh hints, for exploration of new intuitions which may reach beyond old conclusions, set categories, and conventional methods. The books in this series are concerned not only with what is seen and heard, with what the Bible said, but also with what the Bible says and the ways in which seeing and hearing are done.

In putting forth these *Overtures* much remains unsettled. The certainties of the older biblical theology *in service* of dogmatics, as well as of the more recent biblical theology movement *in lieu* of dogmatics, are no longer present. Nor is there on the scene anyone of the stature of a von Rad or a Bultmann to offer a synthesis which commands the theological engagement of a generation and summons the church to a new restatement of the biblical message. In a period characterized by an information explosion the relation of analytic study to attempts at synthesis is unsettled. Also unsettled is the question whether the scholarly canon of the university or the passion of the confessing community provides a language and idiom of discourse, and equally unsettled—and unsettling—is the question whether biblical theology is simply one more specialization in an already fragmented study of scripture or whether it is finally the point of it all.

But much remains clear. Not simply must the community of biblical scholars address fresh issues and articulate new categories for the well-being of our common professional task; equally urgent is the fact that the dominant intellectual tradition of the West seems now to carry less conviction and to satisfy only weakly the new measures of knowing which are among us. We do not know exactly what role the Bible will play in new theological statements or religious postures, nor what questions the Bible can and will address, but *Overtures* will provide a locus where soundings may be taken.

We not only intend that *Overtures* should make contact with people professionally involved in biblical studies, but hope that the series will speak to all who care about the heritage of the biblical tradition. We hope that the volumes will represent the best in a literary and historical study of biblical traditions without canonizing historical archaism. We hope also that the studies will be relevant without losing the mystery of biblical religion's historical distance, and that the studies touch on significant themes, motifs, and symbols of the Bible without losing the rich diversity of the biblical tradition. It is a time for normative literature which is not heavy-handed, but which seriously challenges not only our conclusions but also the shape of our questions.

The treatment of *blessing* by Prof. Westermann is indeed an overture toward new theological possibilities. He offers a full statement here of the theological construct upon which he has been working in various presentations. It is argued that salvation as the substance of biblical faith includes not only *deliverance* but also *blessing*. But it is consistently and singularly deliverance which has been discerned in the Bible and presented in the faith of the church, largely to the neglect of the blessing theme. The present volume effectively recovers that countertheme which has been significant for biblical faith since the work of the Yahwist in ancient Israel. The author is able to show that blessing is also more important in the New Testament than has been generally recognized.

While deliverance is most appropriate to the kerygmatic concerns of the church, it is *blessing* which upholds, sustains, and undergirds all of life. While there may be attention to the main saving "events," it is the gracious, abiding governance of God which underlies such events and provides context for them. Israel's faith is concerned not simply with interventions on the part of God, but with the coherence, reliability, and life-giving power of the created world as ordered by God. It is likely that theology concerned only with deliverance has denied an important resource for communication, for it is blessings in daily life that provide an important arena for theology.

Westermann is able to discern that both in the Old Testament and in the New Testament, there is tension between the old understandings of early religion and the new discernments of faith. In the Old Testament, this tension is between prehistorical *magic* and Israel's notion of *promise*, so that old pre-Israelite nontheological means of blessing are transformed and now utilized for a fresh faith posture. Similarly in the New Testament, the tension is between the old pattern of *Israel's claim* of promise and the *new confession* of Jesus of Nazareth as the blesser and blessing. In both cases, the old and new are held together, so that what is presented does not turn its back on what has been held, even in prefaith affirmation. While deliverance may present what is fresh and peculiar in the Bible, it is blessing that maintains the essential interfaces with life and culture. It is blessing which values the continuities with older teachings, which may be utilized and transformed but not abandoned. Deliverance may suggest that Israel's faith is new. But blessing knowingly recognizes that Israel's faith is rooted in and shaped in important ways by what has gone before.

Westermann is able to carry these insights shrewdly in two remarkable directions. On the one hand, he sees how the faithful practice of blessing in *liturgy* might bring worship close to the reality of life. On the other hand, he sees that blessing keeps the Bible in touch with human experience, even as life becomes more fully *secularized*. Genuinely secularized reality yearns for blessing, for a sign of the overplus of graciousness in the midst of secular experience. It is understanding of blessing which offers a new way to think both about liturgy and about secularization. Indeed, it may be the link between the two. While deliverance is always on the brink of forming a new community discontinuous from the old history, blessing is concerned with the sustenance of life as it is lived in the old history. Westermann offers what may be a quite fresh interfacing between *liturgy and secularization*.

Westermann, recognized as among the most masterful and insightful of Scripture interpreters, invites the reader to fresh categories of interpretation, categories which engage biblical claims fully, but which also engage fully the life most of us live. He offers an enticing overture beyond our conventional ways of discerning biblical faith. His study is precisely what has been envisioned in the presentation of this series of *Overtures*.

WALTER BRUEGGEMANN
JOHN R. DONAHUE, S. J.

Abbreviations

BBB	*Bonner biblische Beiträge*
BEvT	*Beiträge zur evangelischen Theologie*
BHH	*Biblisch-Historisches Handwörterbuch*, ed. Bo Reicke and L. Rost
Bibl.	*Biblica*
BiLi	*Bibel und Liturgie*
BWANT	*Beiträge zur Wissenschaft vom Alten und Neuen Testament*
BZAW	*Beihefte zur Zeitschrift für die alttestamentliche Wissenschaft*
EKL	*Evangelisches Kirchenlexikon*
EvTh	*Evangelische Theologie*
HTR	*Harvard Theological Review*
IDB	*Interpreter's Dictionary of the Bible*, ed. George A. Buttrick
JBL	*Journal of Biblical Literature*
MPTh	*Monatschrift für Pastoraltheologie*
NedTTs	*Nederlands theologisch tijdschrift*
NTSt	*New Testament Studies*
RB	*Revue biblique*
RGG	*Religion in Geschichte und Gegenwart*
RQ	*Römische Quartalschrift für christliche Altertumskunde und Kirchengeschichte*
ThB	*Theologische Blätter*
Theol. Arbeiten	*Theologische Arbeiten*
ThLZ	*Theologische Literaturzeitung*

ThW	*Theologisches Wörterbuch*
TWNT	*Theologisches Wörterbuch zum Neuen Testament*
VT	*Vetus Testamentum*
ZdZ	*Zeichen der Zeit*
ZDMG	*Zeitschrift der deutschen morgenländischen Gesellschaft*
ZNW	*Zeitschrift für die neutestamentliche Wissenschaft*

Preface

As I write this preface, Christmas is approaching and people are wishing each other a "blessed Christmas" or "Christmas blessings." What do we mean in our day when we wish for each other the blessings of this season? Does something really happen, or are we using an empty formula, something left over from an earlier time that has lost its meaning for our day? No one has examined the meaning and function of the benediction in our worship services. Is it a sort of concluding petition, or is it an independent action that has a significance all its own? In addition, there is the question of what relationship exists between the blessing bestowed in the service as an act of worship and the wish for blessing expressed outside the church in ordinary life. Is there any relationship at all? And finally, we must raise the same question with reference to the specific occasions in church life when blessings are bestowed; for example, confirmation in German is called *Einsegnung,* "imparting a blessing." There is so much uncertainty about the significance and the legitimacy of such activities that even within the church their necessity is not clearly or widely recognized or accepted.

These questions call for theological clarification, and that means clarification on the basis of the Bible. But neither systematic nor biblical theologians have shown much interest in blessing; it is an issue that lies off the beaten tracks of theological research, and amazingly few attempts are made to deal with it.

The stimulus to this present study came from the observation that in the Old Testament the concept "salvation" includes both blessing and deliverance, that is, God's activity of blessing and of rescuing his people. It became increasingly clear to me that this concept that includes blessing and deliverance has not been dealt with adequately in terms of the Old Testament context because God's bestowal of blessing is spoken of in ways and in contexts different from those connected with God's work of deliverance. A consequence of this is the observation that God's blessing and what is said of that blessing have a theologically distinct meaning. It is this meaning that I have endeavored to investigate.

Since, as is widely recognized, what the New Testament says about blessing is largely dependent on the Old Testament, I have also raised the question of blessing in the New Testament. The significance of blessing for the church can be established only by a study of what the entire Bible says about it. In the third part of this book I have indicated something of how what we find in the Bible about blessing can be expressed in the worship and other activities of the church. I sincerely hope that my colleagues in the fields of New Testament and practical theology will forgive me if the limits of my understanding have led me to express anything incorrectly, because my investigation of necessity led me in this direction. The only purpose of this invasion of their disciplines is to stimulate new reflection on blessing there as well. We may then see whether an interdisciplinary discussion of this neglected question is possible.

CHAPTER 1

Deliverance and Blessing:

A Look at Biblical Theology

The Old and the New Testaments agree in that each has at its center an account of deliverance. Both proclaim God primarily as the God who saves. In New Testament theology all the characteristic, comprehensive concepts relate to this central point of God's saving action: gospel, sin, grace, life and death, revelation, faith, righteousness. There is general agreement that the divine activity to which the New Testament bears witness, and that which takes place between God and man, can be traced along this one line of God's saving activity in Christ. It is from this line that all central theological concepts are to be understood, and to it that they are to be related.

Following Luther's translation of the Bible, this saving act of God in Jesus Christ is generally called a *Heilstat* or *Heilsgeschehen*—a saving act or event. In the most important passages, Luther translated the Greek *soteria* as *Heil*, for example, Acts 4:12, "And there is salvation [*Heil*] in no one else." No one can deny the significant place of the word *Heil* in the language of theology of the church. It is seen especially in such common compounds as *Heilsgeschichte* (salvation history), *Heilslehre* (doctrine of salvation), *Heilsgewissheit* (assurance of salvation), *Heilsweg* (way of salvation), *Heilsbotschaft* (message of salvation), *Heilsglaube* (saving faith), and so on.

It is therefore striking that in the recent major encyclopedias—*Religion in Geschichte und Gegenwart* and *Evangelisches Kirchenlexikon*—there is no entry for *Heil*. If an adherent of another religion were to consult the best-known Protestant reference works in the German language to find what Christians mean by salvation, he would discover that there is no such entry, not even a dummy entry with cross references to other articles that explain what the word means. Because these works have only a few entries for words compounded with *Heil*, the non-Christian has no way of learning what is meant by the word. If he looks in the encyclopedias for *Rettung* as a word corresponding to the Greek *soteria,* he will find that it is not there either. In the *Evangelisches Kirchenlexikon* there is a cross reference from "Soteriology" to "Christ" and "Christology."

So we are confronted by the situation that the word which is the most widely used term for the real point of Christian belief is neither discussed nor explained in these encyclopedias. Many reasons might be given why this is so. First, in the Christian vocabulary the word *faith* has come to mean that which is be-lieved (*fides quae* in contrast to *fides qua*). Then too, salvation has been so identified with the bringer of salvation that the message of salvation is identified with the message about Christ, thus, soteriology with Christology.

As a result, one no longer asks what we really mean by "salvation." It is assumed that everyone knows. The word is used unthinkingly, uncritically, and usually vaguely, with no clear definition of its meaning. In an address entitled "The Under-standing of Salvation in a Secular Age,"[1] Gerhard Ebeling identi-fies three characteristics of a "true understanding of salvation": (1) "salvation is to be expected only from God"; (2) "salvation takes away the power of death"; (3) "salvation introduces the saving distinction between eschatological and temporal salva-tion." What does he mean when he says that salvation introduces a distinction between two types of salvation? Ebeling does not say what is really meant by "salvation."

The use of the word in an uncritical and imprecise manner has come to be generally accepted, and this usage is assumed to cor-respond to the Greek word *soteria.* That word denotes primarily an act of deliverance and thus it cannot designate the state of having been rescued. This latter meaning is represented in the Latin translations by the word *salus,* which was in turn rendered

1. *Kontexte* 4 (1967) : 5–14.

by the German *Heil*. *Salus* and *Heil* can express only the second meaning of *soteria*; they both express a condition and can in no way describe an act of deliverance.

There is more involved here, however, than the distinction between an event and a state. Originally, neither *salus* nor *Heil* had anything to do with the semantic domain of "rescuing," "redeeming," or "liberating." They refer rather to the state of being "whole," "healthy," "intact." A clear indication of this can be seen in the use of both words as greetings. In this they correspond to the Hebrew words for blessing and peace, because a greeting belongs in the same semantic area as blessing. The Hebrew word *shālōm* is also purely a designation of a state and serves similarly as a greeting.

In the translation of the Greek *soteria* into the Latin *salus* and the German *Heil*, we are dealing then with a shift to another semantic area and thus with a fundamental change in meaning. It is this that is responsible for the contemporary confusion in the use of *Heil*, and the question of what *Heil* should mean for us today must commence with a clarification of this point. What does "salvation" mean—the act of deliverance by Christ, or a new condition that results from this act, or both? Can this new condition be designated by a term that denotes a state of having received a blessing?

Because, first in Latin and then in German, God's action in Christ came to be expressed more and more by terms that depict a condition—and that mean something entirely different from the original—it came about that the distinction was obscured between God's saving acts and God's actions that produced a condition of well-being, that is, between deliverance and blessing. *Salus* and *Heil* were ideally suited to conceal this distinction by including both blessing and deliverance. God's saving activity was reduced to a single dimension.

But this does not represent what the Bible teaches. Does the deliverance that takes place in "salvation history" really remain the same throughout the Bible? In our use of language in all the theological disciplines, we assume that this is the case, but this does not correspond to the Old and New Testament usage. From the beginning to the end of the biblical story, God's two ways of dealing with mankind—deliverance and blessing—are found together. They cannot be reduced to a single concept because, for one reason, they are experienced differently. Deliverance is experienced in events that represent God's intervention. Blessing is a continuing activity of God that is either present or not present. It cannot be experienced in an event any more than can growth or motivation or a decline of strength.

The translation of *soteria* by *salus* and *Heil* resulted in a serious distortion of the biblical data. That which is found in the Bible as something constant, as a condition expressed in blessing, became a secondary feature of God's work of deliverance and thereby transformed the event of deliverance into a condition. The possibility of this was present in *soteria*, in that it can mean both the act of deliverance and its consequences.

Here lies the error that led Western theology to a number of further misinterpretations of and deviations from the message of the Bible. The crucial point is that if what the Bible says about God's dealings with mankind is reduced to a single concept (*soteria—salus—Heil*), it is then possible to reduce these dealings to one dimension and thereby effectively to divorce them from history. This can occur if the salvation so conceived of is expressed in a doctrine of salvation. The saving event then can be spiritualized into an encounter between God and the human soul. Or the saving event can be interpreted in terms of the individual human soul that experiences it. The dogmatic, idealistic, and existential interpretations belong together because in all of them it is presupposed that God's activity with mankind can be subsumed under one concept.

That is not the case in the Bible. The heart of the Bible in both the Old and the New Testaments is history. But this would not be possible if a one-dimensional salvation were involved. If the Bible were only an account of God's salvation and God's judgment, then these two would merely alternate without variation. When the Bible speaks of God's contact with mankind, his blessing is there alongside his deliverance. History comes into being only when both are there together. The element of contingency, essential to historical events, enters the biblical history through the presence together of God's activity in saving and blessing and through their effect on each other. The Bible can be a story because in its reports of God's actions with people these two sides of his activity create an infinite variety of possibilities.

It is God's blessing that provides for the sequence of human births generation after generation, in which all persons are individuals. Their individuality is not wiped out by what they have in common with everyone else. In addition to what they have in common, each one is an individual, whose life history therefore cannot be identical with that of any of the millions of other human beings. It is God's blessing that lets the child grow into a man or woman, that bestows such manifold talents, and that provides physical and spiritual food from so many sources. Without these elements of growth, maturation, and decline, of lesser and greater gifts, of the relations between men and women, there is no real history.

The event of deliverance, the proclamation of the message and its acceptance by faith, saying yes to God in confession, the pronouncement of forgiveness, justification—all these are but momentary occurrences. But the sum total of these moments does not give us history. For them to become history, those things that have continuity must be added—growth and maturation, prospering and succeeding, expanding and contracting, taking root and spreading out.

The distinction between God's action in deliverance and in blessing, or the explication of the proper meaning of blessing alongside deliverance, has far-reaching consequences for the theology of the Old Testament.

We need not conclude that the word *Heil* must be avoided, or even banned from the theological vocabulary, because of its semantic inadequacy. Drawing the distinction allows *Heil* to retain its function and its comprehensive meaning. But it forbids us when speaking of salvation (or of such concepts as salvation history, saving acts, etc.) in theological discussion, and specifically in exegesis, to ignore the question of whether we mean deliverance or blessing, being saved or being blessed. Where necessary for clarity, we will distinguish between the two in translating, but the real issue is not the choice of vocabulary but the recognition of the theological relevance of the difference between God's activity in deliverance and in bestowing blessing.

1. This distinction has first of all an effect on the concept of

history we use in Old Testament research. We can no longer hold that God's activity with his people is to be found only in his "mighty acts." In addition to these acts, experienced in events, God's work with his people includes things manifested not in deeds but in processes that are usually regarded as "unhistorical" —the growth and multiplying of the people and the effects of the forces that preserve their physical life, that is, the threefold blessing of which Deuteronomy speaks, but also growth, prosperity, and success in all their forms.

This coexistence of God's two ways of dealing with his people forces us to revise the terms most used in history. God's history with his people is no longer to be seen only in such documented events as the exodus from Egypt, the occupation of the Promised Land, and the expulsion of their enemies, that is, in events that can be located in time and space. It is also to be found in activity that cannot be dated but that nonetheless has the same degree of historical reality. This leads to a modification of the concept of history. For Israel God controls not only the events of history but also such things as sending rain. During the weeks of a drought, this type of divine activity can attain an eminently historical significance, because the existence of the people depends on it. No concept of history that excludes or ignores God's activity in the world of nature can adequately reflect what occurs in the Old Testament between God and his people.

A well-differentiated concept of history can be seen in the work of the Yahwist, who, by bringing together primeval history, the patriarchal narratives, and the history of God's people, combined three distinct types of happenings into a unified whole. In our use of the word, history begins only with the Exodus, when the nation's history begins. The patriarchal narratives have a different structure that corresponds to the life of a family or a clan and the events that are determinative for it. The activity of God that determines these events is not primarily deliverance but blessing. And the primeval history is characterized by yet another structure; it recounts events involving the world and mankind before the forms of community and existence arose that characterize the present day. As in these three parts of the Yahwistic history the subjects are different—mankind, the family, the nation—so also are the structures in which the events are portrayed different.

In the discussion of Gerhard von Rad's theology of the Old Testament, a central issue was the relationship between the Old Testament account of "God's history with his people" and historical events that could be documented and evaluated by a critical historiography. James M. Robinson[2] deals with this problem in section one of his article, "The Problem of History," and in section two, "The Historicity of Salvation History." In the discussions of the historicity of salvation history, the concern was whether such Old Testament accounts as the sacrifice of Isaac in Genesis 22 were relevant for God's activity with his people even if they could not be established as historical events. This question is seen in another light when we recognize that God's actions with his people include occurrences that by their nature cannot be verified, and certainly not verified as historical. In Jeremiah 14:22, a lament of the people, we read:

> Are there any among the false gods
>   of the nations that can bring rain?
> Or can the heavens give showers?
> Art thou not he, O Lord our God?
>   We set our hope on thee,
>   for thou doest all these things.

The sending of rain is prayed for as something that God does, and it is just as real and just as essential to the existence of the nation as is the defeat of their enemies. Here it is even characterized as an activity of the covenant God. "Remember and do not break thy covenant with us" (Jer. 14:21). The sending of rain is here as much a part of the activity of the God of Israel, the covenant God, as is any historical deed.

A history of God's actions, as recorded in the Old Testament, or a history of salvation, can therefore not be based solely on historical facts in our sense of the word, whether or not they can be shown to be historically factual. "Unhistorical" elements are a necessary part. The line quoted above, "or can the heavens give showers" (i.e., of themselves), shows how far removed this is

---

2. "Heilsgeschichte und Lichtungsgeschichte," *EvTh* 22 (1962) : 113ff.

from our own thinking. We, believers and unbelievers alike, are convinced that the sky (or the clouds) gives rain by itself, and so none of us any longer takes seriously any activity of God in what we call nature. We also think that we can ignore it in our theological thinking. If, however, we hold to what the Old Testament itself says about God's actions on behalf of his people, then it is not possible to have a concept of salvation history that limits God's saving acts to what he does in history.

Nor is it possible to study the Old Testament by using a concept of history for which historically verifiable events are what really took place and for which the basic question is always "Can an event be verified historically and critically as having occurred or not?" To the extent that the Old Testament deals with events of which the text says that God was acting in them, such events by their nature transcend the historically verifiable because they involve an area in which we can neither find nor recognize historical events. A concept of history that has not taken this into account cannot be relevant to the texts of the Old Testament.

2. The distinction between God's saving activity and his bestowal of blessing has significance for the concept of God. The God who saves is the one who comes; the one who blesses is the one who is present (or dwelling or enthroned). It is not possible to restrict God's activity to one or the other of these aspects. It is not possible to portray God only as the one who comes and then to say that because God is coming what the Old Testament says about God is "eschatological," as does Jürgen Moltmann in his *Theology of Hope*. Nor is it possible on the basis of a specific interpretation of the cult to declare that the God who is present is the only God, and then explain God's presence in the sanctuary as the central point of Old Testament theology. In the Old Testament, what is said of God's coming and of his presence belong together. Neither is absorbed by the other; neither negates the other.

(a) On the one side the situation is clear and well known. The God who saves is always the one who comes. That begins in Exodus 3:8 with the deliverance from Egypt, "I have come down to deliver them" (cf. Exod. 15:21), and it extends to Revelation

22:20, "Surely I am coming soon." In the Ark oracle (Num. 10:35–36) we find "Arise, O Lord, and let thy enemies be scattered." And in the psalms of lament the plea for God to intervene is always connected with the plea for God to come. The twofold form of petition, which asks God to be attentive and then to intervene, is the clearest evidence of this connection. The God who rescues (or liberates or helps) is the God who comes. In the praise of God, the epiphany is an especially impressive evidence of this. God appears (comes near) in order to help his beleaguered people (Judg. 5:4–5; Ps. 18; Hab. 3, etc.). In the New Testament the corresponding feature is the epiphany of the Son of God, or his coming as savior.

(b) On the other side the evidence is not so clear or direct. Alongside the epiphanies, which always involve God's activity to rescue (or to judge) his people, there are theophanies, which have a different linguistic form and a different origin and history. In them the place where God appears is a holy site, which is never the case with an epiphany. Many of the theophany accounts justify the establishment of a place as holy. It is from a holy place that blessing is bestowed, and the cultic form of blessing is tied to a holy place. God's being seated on his throne is also a feature of the blessing (Isa. 6; 1 Kings 22; etc.). God as king is the one who bestows blessing (though he does more too), just as the earthly king mediates the blessing.

That God's deliverance and blessing belong together is seen most clearly in the Old Testament in the transition of his people from a nomadic to a settled life. The signs of the God who comes, of God in motion, cease or are united with those of the present God. The ark comes into the temple. The realization that something really changed then in God's actions is expressed clearly in the note in Joshua 5:12 that the manna ceased when they entered the promised land: "And the manna ceased on the morrow, when they ate of the produce of the land; and the people of Israel had manna no more, but ate of the fruit of the land of Canaan that year."

Just as taking the ark into the temple was a sign that God's coming was now one with his giving of blessing, so from then on much was said that brought these two features together in Israel.

We cannot therefore expect to find everywhere a clear distinction. In the prophets, for example, statements about the coming God predominate; but especially Isaiah and Ezekiel, who took up the Jerusalem cult traditions, speak of God as the one who is present, especially on Zion, the holy place of his presence. In Haggai the overwhelming emphasis is on God as the present one, and here it is clearest that the present God is the one who blesses.

It is then not possible to absolutize what is said of the God who comes to judge and to save. There is always a tendency to do so wherever a one-sided emphasis is placed on "the prophetic faith" or "prophetic religion." By the same token, it is not possible to absolutize the God who is present in the cult, as tends to happen wherever there is a one-sided emphasis on the cultic institutions. God's history with his people includes his deeds of deliverance and judgment; it also includes his constant work in their midst as the God who is present.

3. The distinction between God's work of deliverance and his work of blessing has its effect in a total theology of the Old Testament in such a way that God's saving actions can no longer be reduced to soteriological terms because they are not identical with his work of deliverance. An attempt has been made to construct a theology of the Old Testament purely in terms of soteriology (though it is doubtful whether this Christian doctrinal concept is applicable to the data of the Old Testament) by taking the other modes of God's activity and subordinating them to and incorporating them into God's acts of deliverance, which are considered decisive for this theology. What is said about creation especially is interpreted whenever possible in terms of soteriology. As an example, consider von Rad's statement:[3] "This history can be termed salvation history because in its presentation creation was already understood as one of God's saving works." This tendency is seen also in the theological evaluation of the patriarchal narratives, when the concept of promise is given such prominence that the idea of blessing loses its distinctive significance. It is seen also in the interpretation of the prophetic prom-

3. *Die Theologie des Alten Testaments,* 4th ed. (Munich, 1957–60), vol. 2, pp. 380–81.

ises of salvation, when no distinction is made between the proclamation of deliverance and the portrayal of a state of salvation
(blessing).

Throughout the theology of the Old Testament, the question
must at least be raised as to which texts and pericopes belong to
the context of salvation history in the sense of history of deliverance and which, on the contrary, belong to the totally different
context of God's blessing and its history. Then the mutual relationships of these two modes of God's activity, with their varying
interrelationships and their influence on each other in the biblical accounts, must become determinative throughout for the
structure of any theology of the Old Testament.

Such a distinction would result in a more precise treatment of
the events that are significant for this theology and a more careful use of concepts that have been utilized in too general a manner. Let us look at a few examples.

(a) We would have to deal more cautiously with what has
been a too general discussion of the faith of the Old Testament
or faith in the Old Testament. We have grown accustomed to
designating the total relationship of man to God in the Old
Testament as faith, because the central significance of this concept in the New Testament has made "faith" into a general
concept that is often almost identical with "religion," or even
takes the place of the concept of religion. The Old Testament,
however, speaks of faith only in specific, limited contexts, where
it is related to some definite act of God or to a message that is
related to that act. It is sufficient here to mention the very preg-
nant statements that Isaiah makes about faith, and von Rad's
thesis that Isaiah's statements have their origin in the traditions
of the wars of Yahweh.

The Old Testament does not speak of faith in connection with
the blessings God bestows. The grateful acceptance of these blessings is not called faith and is not placed in any relationship with
faith. It is even more striking that in the Old Testament we
never find the word *faith* where creator and creation are spoken
of. We have become accustomed to speaking of the creation faith
in the Old Testament, and we have found no difficulty in taking
everything that the Old Testament says about Creator and crea-

tion as the expression of a creation faith. How is it so easy to do this when the Old Testament itself never does so?

It would first be necessary to show that for the Old Testament the concept of faith really has the same comprehensive significance it has for the New. The relative rareness of the word itself cannot be regarded as decisive. But we would have to show, for example, that what Isaiah meant by "faith" is so unequivocally determinative for the total concept of God in the Old Testament that we have sufficient ground for speaking of "the faith of Israel," "the faith of the prophets," "saving faith," "history of faith," and so on. This would be difficult to do, however, when the Old Testament does not speak at all of any such thing as faith in the Creator, and when God's acts of blessing are never brought into a connection with faith.

It seems to me that the question whether the general, comprehensive concept of faith, which is determinative for the New Testament, can be borrowed as it stands for use in Old Testament studies is especially important for the dialogue between the two Testaments. I want to call attention to the final section of Hans Conzelmann's article "Fragen an Gerhard von Rad"[4] in which he assumes that in discussing the Old Testament it is possible simply to speak of faith in as general and comprehensive a manner as we can in relation to the New Testament. On this basis he inquires into the relationship between the ideas of faith in the two Testaments. His comparison, however, rests on unclarified presuppositions.

(b) The concept of "revelation" is used similarly in a broad, comprehensive manner. In theological language this is seen particularly in the distinction drawn between a saving revelation and a natural revelation or between special and general revelation. Moltmann, in his *Theology of Hope*, has shown how the concept of revelation held by the previous era was largely characterized by this alternative. Such a general concept that embraces the possibilities of a saving revelation and a revelation in creation finds no support in the Old Testament because God's works of creation and of bestowing blessing have no relationship to anything like

4. *EvTh* 3 (1964) : 123–25.

revelation. Everything that we encounter of God's revealing him-self, appearing, letting himself be seen or observed has the char-acteristics of special events that transcend the course of time. God's bestowal of blessing—growth, success, increase, provision—comes as continuing processes and has no need of the extraordi-nary occurrences that we mean by "revelations." It cannot have the nature of revelation, and the use of a concept such as revela-tion to describe God's constant activities is simply not possible in the Old Testament.

(c) In the discussions of the relationship of the Old Testament to the New, the concept "promise" has been used in so general a manner that its contours have become less and less clear. "Prom-ise" as used by Friedrich Baumgärtel on the one hand has almost nothing in common with the way it was used by Walther Zim-merli on the other. What was brought together in these compre-hensive concepts is found in the Old Testament itself in various passages in forms that differ from one another. For instance, the proclamation of salvation that depends on a future event is to be distinguished from a depiction of salvation that points to a state of being blessed. The proclamation is found in the context of God's saving actions, and the depiction is that of God's be-stowal of blessing.

This distinction helps to clarify the so-called prophecy of salva-tion in that within prophecies so designated we must separate those that announce an act of deliverance, as Isaiah 7 proclaims the rescue of Jerusalem from the foes who are threatening it, and those that describe a condition, such as Isaiah 2, a thoroughly different picture. To call both of these passages "oracles of sal-vation" does not adequately identify them.

4. The distinction between God's acts of deliverance and those of blessing enables us to bring together the extremely different conceptions of Israelite worship current today. On the one hand, Israel's worship is seen as bearing the stamp of a non-Israelite understanding of cult, and on the other the amphictyonic cult is seen as worship in the covenant relationship, a pure celebration of God's saving deeds for Israel. We can see in this clear-cut con-trast that these analyses of worship in Israel are based in the first case on a one-sided emphasis on the bestowal of blessing, and in

the other on deliverance. Neither camp realizes that in the Old Testament these two modes of God's activity for his people stand side by side and that in none of the combinations possible between them does either completely eliminate the other. This indicates that both must have been a part of Israelite worship. There is ample material to support this conclusion.

The psalms are a good example of how the two belong together. The distinctive nature of the psalms in contrast to neighboring cultures is seen in the great extent to which history is presented in them. But the psalms are not just history. The psalms of blessing, the Zion psalms, and the pilgrimage psalms have as their focal point the sanctuary and the blessings bestowed there. The distinction can be readily seen in the two categories of songs of praise. The praise of God that responds to God's deeds is found in Israel as declarative praise. It is related only to events that God performs for his people as a whole or individually, and these deeds call forth this praise. Descriptive praise (the hymn), on the other hand, is more comprehensive. It describes the whole of God's actions and being, including God's bestowal of blessing and his work of creation. In the existence of these two forms side by side, we can see the awareness of the distinction between God's deliverance and his blessings.

5. The distinction is also observable in the office of the mediator of salvation. The priest is primarily the mediator of God's continuous blessing, while the charismatic leader and the prophet mediate God's activity through events. There seems to be no need to carry this further. The significance of this distinction for Old Testament theology should be clear by now.

CHAPTER 2

Blessing in the Bible

Our starting point for an investigation of the meaning and significance of blessing in the Bible must be the recognition that in existing research in both Testaments the distinctive characteristics of blessing and of God's bestowal of blessing have scarcely been noted at all. In part this can be explained in terms of what has been said in Chapter 1 about deliverance and blessing. Theologies of the Old and New Testaments take almost no notice of blessing and God's role in it. None of the recent theologies assigns it a distinctive significance in the whole range of the dealings between God and man.

BLESSING IN OLD TESTAMENT THEOLOGIES AND THE HISTORY OF RELIGION

Older works (e.g., those of Dillmann, Schultz, Marti, Smend, and Kittel) do not deal with blessing. The same is true of the two-volume work of Sellin, who treated the history of religion and Old Testament theology separately. Walther Eichrodt occasionally mentions blessing in his theology. He does not relate it to its larger context, but there is a brief treatment that brings together some comments on blessing in Part 3 in a footnote.[1] Except for a few comments, blessing is not dealt with in the extensive Old Testament theologies of Eduard König and O. Procksch. Even in Theodorus C. Vriezen's theology it is mentioned only a few times in passing. It is remarkable that even in those Old Testament theologies that give an extensive portrayal of cult, blessing is not

---

1. Walther Eichrodt, *Die Theologie des Alten Testaments*, 3 vols. (Leipzig, 1933–39).

treated but merely mentioned. Only in Bernhard Stade's 1905 work did I find a single heading: "Blessing, Curse, Oath."

In the table of contents of Gerhard von Rad's theology, the word *blessing* is not to be found in either part of the work. In the index to volume one a list of passages is given for blessing, and in the index to volume two, one passage. In those passages blessing is mentioned but the theme is never developed. As a theological concept, blessing has for von Rad, as for all his predecessors, little if any significance. In a few passages he attacks Johannes Pedersen and his understanding of blessing.[2]

This fact is especially striking when we recall that von Rad wrote commentaries on the two Old Testament books in which the concept of blessing occurs most frequently and obviously has great significance—Genesis and Deuteronomy (both commentaries in the series Das Alte Testament Deutsch). No one can deny that in Genesis 12–50 and in the framework of Deuteronomy, blessing is one of the central concepts. How then can we explain the fact that von Rad did not assign any importance to this concept in his theology?

The answer can only be that in these two books and also throughout the Old Testament, von Rad subsumed the concept "blessing" under that of salvation (*Heil*). He assumed that God's saving deeds and his acts of blessing together constitute God's activity as savior. In Genesis 12:1–3 he saw the "Beginning of Salvation History"[3] and in Exodus 3ff. its continuation, even though in the former only God's blessing is spoken of and in the latter only God's deliverance. For von Rad there is no problem. God's saving actions include deliverance and blessing and there is no tension between them. He consistently makes use of the comprehensive concept of salvation (*Heil* and its compounds), by which he primarily means God's acts of deliverance but in which God's bestowal of blessing is included with no feeling of tension. In the section "The Earliest Reports of Salvation History"[4] salvation, as the subject of this history, is presented as a

2. Gerhard von Rad, *Die Theologie des Alten Testaments*, 4th ed. (Munich, 1957–60), vol. 1, p. 267, n. 64.
3. Ibid., p. 177.
4. Ibid., pp. 127–34.

unity; it appears irrelevant that the texts speak at times of deliverance and at other times of blessing. The same is true of the summary at the end of volume two," The Old Testament History of Salvation in the Light of Its Fulfillment in the New Testament."[5] God's blessing is not even mentioned; it is included as a part of God's deliverance of his people or his saving deeds. It is thus clear that in the question of the relationship between the two Testaments, blessing is assigned no role. When the presentations of salvation in the two Testaments are brought together, that of the New Testament is understood purely in soteriological terms. This is the only theme used in determining the relationship between the two.

Ludwig Köhler is the only scholar to see the meaning of the basic difference between deliverance and blessing.[6] He saw that the occupation of the land produced a distinctive change in what was said about God and his modes of activity.

> Does Yahweh also bestow possessions and prosperity? . . . The new homeland cannot remain without gods. . . . Yahweh protects, and has done so since the Exodus, including the move into Canaan. He has only one history. . . . But possession, and especially growth and prosperity, require continuous activity, a lasting blessing. In place of protection . . . there is now blessing that is constant and active. This is a highly significant change.

This statement recognizes the difference between the momentary nature of deliverance as an event and the continuous nature of blessing, and thus also the significance of the occupation of the land, in which the God who gives deliverance also becomes the one who gives blessing. Although this insight did not affect the structure of Köhler's Old Testament theology, and its implications were not developed, it is there nonetheless.

This significance was rediscovered in the field of history of religion, especially by Johannes Pedersen in his *Israel: Its Life and Culture*, where an entire chapter is devoted to a detailed discussion of blessing; by Sigmund Mowinckel in *Psalmenstudien V*; and by Johannes Hempel in a work on blessing and curse.

5. Ibid., vol. 2, pp. 380–412.
6. *Die Theologie des Alten Testaments* (1947), pp. 54ff.

I will summarize succinctly Pedersen's discussion,[7] since it is
highly important for Old Testament studies. The chapter begins
with a discussion of the soul, a presupposition for Pedersen's understanding of blessing. As a translation of the Hebrew *nephesh*,
"soul" is seen as expressing the person's total state of being alive.
The soul is a totality, filled with power. This power lets the soul
grow and prosper so that it can maintain itself and do its work in
the world. This vital power, without which no living being can
exist, the Israelites called *berākhāh*, "blessing." Blessing is both
internal and external—the inner power of the soul and the good
fortune that produces that power. Everything that has vitality
also has blessing, because blessing is vitality.

Blessing manifests itself in widely differing ways. It is primarily
the power of fertility, an understanding of blessing that remained
constant through the centuries. This is the specific meaning of
the concept of blessing and is the meaning in Genesis 1:22, 28.
Above all, this meaning unfolds in the patriarchal narratives,
and it is the main motif in the Abraham stories. We find repeatedly the promise that God will multiply his descendants "as the
stars of heaven." Thus the real meaning of blessing is having
many descendants. A man who has descendants is said to have a
soul that flourishes and grows; he has a "house." Blessing is identical with the survival of the family.

Blessing is also the power of fruitfulness in a wider sense of
fertility in the family, in farming, in raising cattle and sheep.
It is seen again and again that blessing is fertility. Blessing is the
center of life; it is life itself and it includes all phases of life.
It is the positive vital power, which for the people of Israel is
manifest above all in fertility.

Blessing can be extended to include the power to defeat one's
enemies (Gen. 24:60; 27:29). The Balaam oracles promise success in warfare (Num. 24:17–18). And in the prophecies to the
tribes, this power is especially given to Judah (Deut. 33:7) and
Joseph (Gen. 49:22–26).

The total "soul" of a person embraces everything within the
circle of his life, everything around him. If his soul is strong it

---

7. Johannes Pedersen, *Israel: Its Life and Culture* (London, 1926), vols. 1–2,
pp. 162–212, "The Blessing"; see also the index to vols. 3–4.

must leave an impression on all his undertakings. It is not only the family of one who is rich in blessing that shares in the blessing; in foreign lands Jacob and Joseph had the power to spread blessing around them. The one who possesses blessing is *barukh*, full of *berākhāh*. Power must flow out from him in every direction. This power of blessing has "spiritual" as well as "physical" effects. It is seen in the counsel a man gives, as this already implies the deed (Isa. 9:5; 11:2; 2 Sam. 15:34). Blessing is the soul's power that produces all progress (*salah*). This means it is related to wisdom ("With God are wisdom and might," Job 12:13). Wisdom, like blessing, is the power to accomplish, to succeed. Note the verb *hiskil*, which can mean "have insight" as well as "succeed." Thus, blessing means having vital power in its deepest, most comprehensive sense.

A king must receive the greatest blessing in order that the whole nation can draw blessing from him (1 Sam. 16:18). Here the external manifestation is included. David is the prototype of the king who has been blessed, and the blessing is the issue in the conflict between David and Saul.

The act of blessing, *bērēkh*, means imparting vital power to another person. The one who blesses gives the other person something of his own soul. The handing on of blessing from father to son is a result of its being a power of the soul. It must continue in the family because the family is a spiritual unit.

Interpersonal relations are not possible without blessing. When people meet, they bless each other. For Israel, the greeting was a form that contained a deep reality; it established or confirmed a spiritual community. This means it is the same as giving a blessing and it is necessary for the establishment of a relationship. When friends part they bless each other in order to strengthen the friendship. When God's messenger greets Gideon, "The Lord is with you" (Judg. 6:12), words that are another expression of blessing, Gideon's power is recognized as the power of God. Large gatherings, cultic or not, must be concluded with a blessing, so that each individual may take with him the power of the community.

In general, blessing must be reciprocal. Even inferiors may bless their superiors. By so doing, they confirm the blessing that the superior possesses and contribute to its increase (Job 31:20).

Blessing includes the paying of respect (Judg. 5:24). Thus, the king is blessed by his subjects and Yahweh is blessed (i.e., praised) by his people. Here we see how the two meanings of *bērēkh*, to bless and to praise, belong together.

Pedersen's presentation has its limitations in that it lists the phenomena in a rather arbitrary manner without seeking any order, any historical or systematic point of view, or even a point of view in terms of tradition history. He also uses an arbitrary terminology that is not always convincing. So to a certain extent Pedersen has merely accumulated the raw materials. This criticism, however, does not alter the fact that he was the first to recognize the distinctive significance of what the Old Testament says about blessing and thus its theological relevance. He shows conclusively that throughout the Old Testament (he developed a large number of passages, of which I have cited only a few) blessing and the bestowal of blessing constitute an essential part of what occurs there.

In his *Psalmenstudien*, which had such far-reaching effect on Psalm research, Mowinckel also gave a new presentation of the significance of blessing.[8] There is no need to give his ideas here because he explicitly says in his introduction that he is following Pedersen. Mowinckel summarized his concept of blessing in *Religion und Kultus*.[9] His starting place is the significance of blessing for cultic practices.

> All worship reached its culmination in the priestly words of blessing. It was in order to receive blessing and make it secure in all its forms, that Israel, as a community and also as individuals, went to the sanctuary and took part in the worship offered there.

> Through worship and all its rites, blessing was achieved, made secure, and increased for individuals and for the community.

> Blessing includes that which we call material as well as the spiritual. But first and foremost, blessing is life, health, and fertility for the people, their cattle, their fields. . . . Blessing is the basic power of life itself.

8. *Psalmenstudien* 1–6 (Kristiania, 1921–24), vol. 6, see esp. the section "Segen und Fluch in Israels Kult und Psalmendichtung."

9. 1953, pp. 64–66.

Blessing is a capability of the soul, a power that lives in the clan and in its members. The normal, "just" ("righteous") man is also the one who is blessed, and from his blessing, blessing flows out to all those who belong together with him. The clan lives by the blessing of its head, and the nation by that of its king. But they have this power only because of their relationship with Yahweh and because they preserve this relationship properly and renew it in the cult. For Israel, the one blessed is no longer the one who has mana; it is the one who is blessed by Yahweh; the power that brings blessing is the "name of Yahweh."

Mowinckel notes also the connection between blessing and God's work as creator:

> Because life and the powers of life were universally regarded as the most mysterious, awe-inspiring, and important of all reality, they were included in the sphere of holiness, of religion. Life, the power of life, and blessing came to be regarded as holy because they have their origin in the Holy, in the Deity. God is the creator and pre-server of life. This thought has spread throughout the whole earth, even among the most primitive religions. . . . Israel at a very early time borrowed the concept of the creator God and applied it to Yahweh. Yahweh creates life, continually creates the world, and at one time brought the world into being. In the cult each Israelite encounters Yahweh as the one who creates and bestows life and blessing and by so doing upholds the world.[10]

In this discussion the relation of blessing to the cult is strongly emphasized. What the Old Testament says about God's blessing goes far beyond the cult, but Mowinckel did not make this clear. One gets the impression that Pedersen, to whom he often refers, expressed many things in more detail and with more precision. In any case, however, Mowinckel clearly recognized the distinctive nature of what the Old Testament says about blessing.

While Mowinckel begins with the cult and places cultic bless-ings at the center of his discussion, in keeping with his basic view that cult and religion stand in the closest relationship to each other, Johannes Hempel, in his *Die israelischen Anschauungen von Segen und Fluch im Lichte altorientalischer Parallelen*,[11] represents another school of thought, which is especially inter-ested in the evolution from the level of magic to that of ethical

10. Ibid., pp. 55–56.
11. *ZDMG*, N.S. 4.

religion and which is based more on the documents of the religions than on cultic procedures. Hempel's starting point is the assumption that the Old Testament concepts of blessing and curse betray their origins in the practices of primitive magic (p. 20) ; his agreement with Mowinckel is obvious. The origins in magic (pp. 23–47) are evident in the similarity to magical spells and in the union of word and action. "Blessing and curse share with magic an unconditional and inevitable efficacy" (p. 26). "In addition, blessing and curse are contagious to people, animals, and objects" (p. 29)'. Fertility, prosperity, and well-being flow from a king to his land and his people (Babylonian royal inscriptions).

Part 2 of Hempel's work deals with the content of blessing (pp. 47–59). Blessing means life and prosperity. In Akkadian and Arabian texts, too, we find the power of life and reproduction, long life and many descendants, as the content of blessing. This power then is extended to include success in general. The word *shālōm* is the best illustration of how blessing comes to include everything—freedom from threats and dangers, the possession of quiet security, good fortune and well-being to the greatest extent conceivable. In the exchange of greetings, each wishes the other *shālōm*.

Part 3, "Intercession and Prayer for Revenge" (pp. 60–94), presents the significant transition in which blessing and curse in Israel are removed from the realm of magic and are subordinated to God, becoming in the process a part of prayer. The concentration of power in Yahweh's hands is seen in the restrictions placed on human power.

Part 4, "Blessing and Curse as Activities of Yahweh" (pp. 95–109), carries this development further. "That which primitive religion accepts as given and which cultic religion regulates and systematizes in order to protect and serve the nation and the individual, ethical prophetic religion removes entirely from the realm of magic and ceremony and thus prepares the way for the New Testament view of blessing and curse" (p. 95).

It is instructive to compare Mowinckel's position with that of Hempel. The latter adheres strictly to an upward development in three stages: primitive religion, cultic religion, and ethical, prophetic religion. The world view that lies behind this concept is obvious. In Mowinckel we can see traces of an evolutionary view, but there is no such unequivocal upward movement. Since for Mowinckel religion is cultic religion, he does not deal with Hempel's third stage, or at least does not regard it as a developmental step. As a result, the pattern of development disappears. Mowinckel is more interested in the phenomenological meaning of blessing than in the history of how the concept developed. As a result, the essential thing for Mowinckel from the beginning of Israel's history to its end is the cultic impartation of blessing as the power of life.

Clearly, both scholars have a correct point of view, but each overstresses his own position. Neither position, however, presents the significance that the history of blessing in the Old Testament had for the history of God's dealings with his people.

This present work is an initial attempt at a portrayal of that significance. It can only be a general view sketched with broad strokes, without developing the details. We shall begin with the New Testament and proceed from what is provisionally established there back to the Old Testament, in order to return once more in conclusion to the New Testament and examine, in the light of our study, what meaning blessing has there. We are concerned with the meaning of blessing in the whole Bible, and a major concern of this work is to demonstrate that the study of the Old Testament is a necessary prerequisite for understanding blessing in the New Testament.[12]

---

12. It might be asked whether the study of blessing in the Old Testament should not be combined with the study of curses. A number of the bibliographical references cited above investigate blessing and curse together. From the point of view of the history of religion this is certainly correct. In the Old Testament, as elsewhere, blessing and curse are found together, especially in Deuteronomy, e.g., chs. 27 and 28. A comprehensive study of blessing would then require investigation of the relationship of blessing and curse to each other.

In the present study, however, this has deliberately not been done because it would require an extensive study of the pronouncing of curses and also because in the Old Testament blessing and curse by no means always parallel each other. Blessing underwent a totally different development. Quite early blessing was brought into a relationship with the activity of Yahweh, the God of Israel (see the section about blessing in the Yahwist document and in the Balaam oracles on pp. 49ff.), but curse was never placed in such direct relation to Yahweh's work. The Old Testament speaks frequently and in varied contexts of Yahweh's activity in bestowing blessing, but nowhere does it speak of the curse of Yahweh or of Yahweh's putting a curse on someone or

BLESSING IN THE NEW TESTAMENT:
A PRELIMINARY SURVEY

In speaking of blessing in the New Testament it must be kept in mind that "the New Testament view of blessing and curse is closely related to the Old Testament and to Judaism."[13] We cannot then expect to find somewhere in the New Testament a thematic treatment of blessing, or even to find that blessing is brought into a relationship with the central theme of the New Testament. Blessing is spoken of without reflection as something that is known and that undeniably belongs there. No question is raised as to its meaning, and it is not regarded as a problem to be investigated.

The word *blessing* does not occur often in the New Testament. The stem *eulog-* is found 68 times, of which 40 occurrences have the meaning of praise, leaving 28 that signify blessing. Some of these are quotations or paraphrases of Old Testament passages that mention the blessing of the patriarchs. In one instance the word has the concept's original meaning of the power of growth (Heb. 6:7–8). A survey of the passages at once reveals two differing usages. In one, the concept of blessing has been modified to mean more or less specifically God's saving deeds in Christ, for example, Galatians 3:8–9, 14; Acts 3:25–26; Ephesians 1:3. In another group of passages, blessing functions in a way completely determined by the Old Testament; these passages are found in the Gospels and in the letter to the Hebrews.

The Gospels report that Jesus blessed the little children (Mark 10:13–16 and the parallel passages). He pronounces a blessing at

---

something. Instead of speaking of Yahweh's curse, the Old Testament tells of his judgment and punishment. That is to say that in Israel the curse was never theologized the way blessing was.

13. U. Link, "Segen und Fluch im NT," *EKL* 3: 919. On blessing in the New Testament see the following lexicon articles: Hermann W. Beyer, *ThW* 2: 759–63; Walter J. Harrelson, "Blessings and Cursings," *IDB* 1: 446–48; Helmut Köster, *RGG*[3] 5: 1651–52; U. Link, "Segen und Fluch im NT," *EKL* 3: 919–20. See also the following: L. Brun, *Segen und Fluch im Urchristentum* (Oslo, 1932) ; Wolfgang Schenk, "Der Segen im NT: Eine begriffsanalytische Studie," in *Theol. Arbeiten* 15 (1967). For general works on blessing see: Peter Brunner, *Leiturgia* 1 (1954) : 200–202; idem, "Der Segen als dogmatisches und liturgisches Problem," in *Pro Ecclesia* 2 (1966) : 339–51; Ernst Klessmann, "Was heisst Segen nach der Heiligen Schrift?" in *MPTh* 48 (1959) : 26ff. Further literature is listed in Schenk's work cited above.

a meal (Mark 6:41 and parallels; Mark 8:6–7 and parallels). He pronounces the blessing at the Last Supper (Mark 14:22 and parallels; 1 Cor. 10:16). Before he ascends to heaven he blesses his disciples (Luke 24:50–51). He exhorts his disciples to bless those who curse them (Luke 6:28). In none of these passages is there any particular emphasis on blessing, but there is such an emphasis in the mission of the disciples (Matt. 10 and parallels). They are sent out not only with a message but also with the instruction to greet others with a blessing. This passage indicates that the effect of the blessing was a part of what the disciples were to proclaim.

It would be easy to assert that Jesus' commission to the disciples in Matthew 10 has such deep roots in the Jewish soil from which the Gospels grew that it must be understood in terms of that soil; the post-Easter Christian community would thus have been unable to find anything of theological relevance in such a text. It can also be asserted, however, that according to the book of Acts the blessing attached to the commission in Matthew 10 can actually be seen in the career of the messengers of Jesus Christ in the world. In Acts the accounts of greetings and blessings when the apostles arrived somewhere or took their departure are so framed that they cannot be conceived of without these greetings. The same may be said of the Epistles, even though Paul did not simply use stereotyped phrases in his letters but consciously worded his introductory and concluding greetings in a manner appropriate to the situation of those to whom he was writing. Even if it can be said that Paul regarded these greetings as essential components of his letters, weight must be given to the facts that formulas of greeting and blessing in the New Testament letters follow the then-current epistolary style and that therefore nothing specifically Christian is intended or indeed can be expressed in them. Consequently, we can affirm that although in the greetings and pronouncements of blessing in the New Testament there is a continuity with what had been said before about blessing, it is not possible to derive from them a specific definition of blessing.

This survey, which has been limited to the use of the term itself, shows that in the New Testament, blessing does not have any marked significance. It is spoken of as something that is recognized and well known, but it is never the subject of theological reflection, and the act of bestowing a blessing never becomes a prominent or specific institution. Blessing is prominent only in the mission of the disciples. It will be necessary later in this study to explain why this is so.

When we compare the occurrence and the meaning of the concept of blessing and the bestowal of blessing in the Old Testament and in the New, there is no question that while blessing had great significance in the Old Testament, and underwent a complex development, in the New Testament it lost its significance to such a degree that scholars can assert that it has lost there all its importance. Wolfgang Schenk, whose work will be examined later, took this position. But there is a problem here. If this is the case, how was it possible for blessing to take on any significance in the Christian church?

Blessing is found not only in worship and the many specific rituals of blessing in the church but also in the fine arts, which demonstrate how deeply rooted was the concept that Christ was not only the one who saves, the *sōtēr*, but also the one who blesses. This can be seen throughout church history, from the earliest representations of Christ down to those of the nineteenth and twentieth centuries. In all epochs the Christ is portrayed not only as the one who was crucified but also as the one who blesses.

And what is the biblical justification for blessing in the life and work of the church if the New Testament basis is so small? Since it is no longer adequate to find a basis in isolated passages, we must inquire into the meaning of blessing for the whole New Testament and into its relation to the center of the New Testament, the message of salvation in Christ. This question cannot be answered in terms of the New Testament alone; it must be answered on the basis of the entire Bible.

THE MEANING OF BLESSING IN THE OLD TESTAMENT[14]

A sketch of Friedrich Horst's "Segen und Segenshandlungen in der Bibel"[15] may serve as an example of studies along this line.

14. In addition to the works of Pedersen, Mowinckel, and Hempel mentioned above, the following should be noted: Jean-Paul Audet, "Esquisse historique du genre littéraire de la bénédiction juive de l'eucharistie chrétienne," *RB* 65 (1958) : 371–99; Hermann W. Beyer, "Segen und Segnen im Alten Testa-

Horst begins by asserting that "the meaning of blessing in the Bible has been largely explained," and he refers to the works of Pedersen, Hempel, and Beyer. He also refers briefly to the background in the history of religion. "In contrast to the Greek world, the Ancient Near East, especially the area influenced by Akkadian culture, had a highly developed concept of blessing (*karabu*) ." His starting point, however, is problematical in that he does not examine the far-reaching contrasts between Pedersen and Hempel (and Mowinckel, whom he does not mention) and especially in that he feels he can construct his subsequent biblical and theological discussion on the basis of what these scholars say about the meaning of blessing in the history of religion.

Horst summarizes under five headings the Old Testament statements about blessing (pp. 24–26) :

1. When is blessing given? On such occasions as exchange of greetings, weddings, just before dying, at the beginning of a reign, during worship, and so on.

2. How is blessing bestowed? In word and action; the various activities and formulas are enumerated.

3. What is the content of the blessing? Blessing gives the power to live, the intensification of life, fertility. For Israel blessing took on its meaning at the time of its occupation of the Promised Land.

4. Who receives such blessing? God blesses human beings and, for their sake only, other beings. Election and blessing are closely related.

5. Who bestows blessing? God. It is his name alone that gives a blessing its power. People need a special endowment to bestow blessing, and blessing became a privilege of the priests.

---

ment," *ThW* 2: 752–57; E. J. Bickermann, "Bénédiction et prière," *RB* 69 (1962) : 524–32; Johannes Hempel, *RGG*2 5: 391ff.; Friedrich Horst, "Segen und Fluch: II Im A.T.," *RGG*3 5: 1649–51; idem, "Segen und Segenshandlungen in der Bibel," *EvTh* 7 (1947/48) : 23–37; H. Junker, "Segen als heilsgeschichtliches Motivwort im AT," *BEvT* 12–31 (1959) : 548–58; J. Kroll, "Segen," *BiLi* 35 (1962) : 359–63; A. Murtonen, "The Use and Meaning of the Words *lebarek* and *berakhah* in the OT," *VT* 9 (1959) : 158–77; J. Scharbert, " 'Fluchen' und 'Segnen' im AT," *BibLeb* 39 (1958) : 1–26; idem, "Solidarität in Fluch und Segen im AT und in seiner Umwelt," *BBB* 14 (1958) ; Claus Westermann, "Segen und Fluch, II: AT," *EKL* 3: 917–20; idem, "Frage nach dem Segen," *ZdZ* 11 (1957) : 244–53.

15. Cited above, n. 14.

Bringing together in these five questions the Old Testament statements on blessing has value in that it assembles material from quite different contexts. Horst's work can thus be seen as a supplement to my own. But his article has nothing to say in reference to the basic theological questions raised by the biblical phenomenon of blessing. His study is limited in this regard because it treats all the material on the same level and scarcely touches on the extensive changes that took place in the understanding of blessing.

First I shall present a general survey of the issue, which presupposes the material in the introductory chapter. It would be a perversion of the biblical data to reduce God's dealings with his people to the one concept "salvation."[16] In the Old Testament we must distinguish between these two activities of God. The history of God's dealings with his people must show the relations between blessing and salvation, but also the things that distinguish them from each other.

It is not possible to restrict our study to the occurrence of the various forms of the root *brk*. That is the starting point, but since the terminology can also represent the state of being blessed, descriptions of that state, even where the terminology does not occur, are to be included. This is the case, for example, where blessing is portrayed in terms of salvation, in the presentation of Job as one who had been blessed, and also in the themes of the Jacob-Esau cycle in the patriarchal narrative, where the contrasting destinies of the brother who is blessed and the one who is not are given. Where blessing is spoken of, there develops a specific vocabulary in which such terms as *success, succeed, presence of God,* and *peace* recur. It is therefore possible to speak—cautiously and within limits—of a language of blessing, of a semantic domain containing expressions that often recur when the blessedness of a person or a group is depicted. Pedersen

---

16. This is done also by Junker in his work cited in n. 14. He regards blessing as a motif of salvation history (a) where the content of blessing is seen as a comprehensive expression of salvation and (b) when the totality of those under God's saving purpose are the recipients of the blessing. Salvation history is then interpreted as the working out of God's blessing. This merging of salvation and blessing is an outstanding example of the usage of the terms in such a way as to reduce to the vanishing point the distinctive features of God's activities of blessing and deliverance.

and Hempel called attention to this domain. Hempel found the content of blessing "summed up best in the concept *shālōm.*"[17] This is not correct; a distinction must be made. Blessing, *berākhāh,* is the power of growth vertically, from generation to generation (rightly understood as such by Pedersen); *shālōm* is the well-being of a community horizontally. This distinction is specifically followed in the patriarchal narratives. In the Abraham cycle the issue is the continuity from one generation to the next because Abraham is given (and keeps) a son. The Jacob cycle deals with two brothers, one blessed and one not. The Joseph narrative deals with the well-being, the *shālōm,* of a community; it starts with a rupture of relationships and ends with the restoration of the welfare of the community. So in this narrative the motif is rightly expressed as *shālōm.*

These examples demonstrate that in the area of God's bestowal of blessing or in that of blessing in general there is a wealth of specific terms, specific phrases, specific theological questions that have nothing at all to do with salvation history in the sense of a history that begins with God's act of deliverance and is determined by that act. It is thus justifiable to speak of a "theology of blessing" insofar as this means speaking of God in the light of blessing and of God's bestowal of blessing.

IN THE HISTORICAL BOOKS OF THE OLD TESTAMENT

In the Pentateuch, the books Exodus through Numbers present the account of God's saving deeds by which he established his people in history. The two books that precede and follow— Genesis and Deuteronomy—are chiefly concerned with the concept of the blessing that God bestows on his people. In these two books the words *bless* and *blessing* occur more frequently than anywhere else in the Old Testament. In the primeval history (Gen. 1–11) blessing is found in the context of creation and extends to all living creatures. In the stories of the patriarchs (Gen. 12–50) blessing operates in the family or clan, and in Deuteronomy in the nation. The framework of Deuteronomy deals with the reception of God's blessing in the land he has promised his

17. *Die israelischen Anschauungen von Segen und Fluch, ZDMG,* N.S. 4: 51; adopted by Beyer, *ThW* 2: 753.

people. The patriarchal narratives speak of blessing in a wide variety of ways. Its importance becomes apparent in the prologue (Gen. 12:1–3), where the root *brk* occurs five times. The promise of blessing is a motif that permeates these narratives, and the bestowal of blessing, often by a father blessing his child, occurs frequently. The entire cycle of Jacob-Esau stories (Gen. 25–36) is concerned with the meaning of blessing. In the primeval history, blessing is involved not only where the term occurs (Gen. 1:22, 28, etc.; only in P); since blessing here signifies fertility, the genealogies also represent God's activity of granting blessing. Blessing is realized in the succession of generations.

The placing of the history of deliverance (Exodus to Numbers) in a framework of the two books where blessing is the dominant theme is important because it shows that the arrangement of the Pentateuch, the Torah, expresses the close relationship between God's saving activity and the blessing he bestows. There is at least a hint of a wider framework. In the primeval history God's blessing is universal, and this corresponds to the book of Revelation, that great apocalyptic drama of peace where once again the vocabulary of blessing is used and God's blessing is universal. In the Deuteronomic history, the introductory passages of which are parts of Deuteronomy, the distinction cannot be drawn so sharply, but here is the central account of God's work of saving and judging, and it is always in some way accompanied by and brought into relation with the bestowal of blessing. Aside from the continuation of the Deuteronomic themes, the theology of blessing centers in the two institutions that were determinative for the settled life of Israel—kingship and temple. Both are essentially concerned with God's constant activity.[18] Although the king was sent first to save Israel, he is over the decades the bearer and mediator of blessing. The temple is the place where blessing is imparted to the whole nation and to the entire land.[19]

---

18. Walter J. Harrelson, "Blessings and Cursings," *IDB* 1: 446. "After the establishment of the Jerusalem cultus the powers of blessing and cursing were centered in the king, the priesthood of the royal cult and the cult prophets."

19. Solomon's prayer at the dedication of the temple (1 Kings 8) is a magnificent and profound combining of the theology of blessing inherent in the temple with the theology of salvation that developed in the history of God's activities with his people. The drama of peril and deliverance, sin and for-

The relationship of blessing to kingship deserves separate investigation. The thesis of sacral kingship, represented mainly by Scandinavian (e.g., George Widengren) and English scholars (Hooke and his school), has been widely refuted as not applicable for Israel (Martin Noth and many others), but the question still remains as to what it means that in Israel too the king was the mediator of blessing. To be sure, this function was never prominent in Israel and it declined in importance, but there is no denying that it was there, as is shown by the Nathan oracle and its influence on the messianic promises. Pedersen is surely right in claiming (see above) that the heart of the conflict between Saul and David was that one had God's blessing and that the other was losing the power of that blessing. In the account of the struggles over the succession to David's throne, two of the three passages that speak of Yahweh's work refer to God's blessing. In 2 Samuel 12:24 we read: "And she bore a son, and he called his name Solomon. And the Lord loved him."[20] This says that Solomon will be blessed, and the context shows that Yahweh acted with complete freedom in making him the bearer of blessing. And 2 Samuel 17:14 makes clear what happened in Absalom's council of war: "For the Lord had ordained to defeat the good counsel of Ahithophel, so that the Lord might bring evil upon Absalom." The decision was made to choose one counsel over another, and the giving of counsel is a place where blessing is active (so Pedersen, in reference to this passage, see above). Much as was the case in the Balaam pericope, Yahweh exercises in sovereign freedom the power inherent in counsel to accomplish his work in history. In the third passage, 2 Samuel 11:27, an entirely different side of God's activity is seen—the responsibility of men, even the king, for their sin: "But the thing that David

---

giveness is portrayed in Solomon's prayer (vv. 22–53) and explicitly related to God's original act of deliverance, the exodus from Egypt. But Solomon's prayer connects this drama with a totally different activity, the blessing that flows from the temple (vv. 14, 54, in both cases expanded into praise of God). It should be noted that the presentation of the sacrifice occurs only later (vv. 62–65). The significant act of the dedication is the blessing. Note too that here it is still the king who bestows blessing, through whom God blesses his people. This recalls Gen. 14:17–24, where the priest-king of "Salem" (Jerusalem) blesses Abraham.

20. See Gerhard von Rad, "Der Anfang der Geschichtsschreibung im alten Israel," *ThB* 8: 181–84.

had done displeased the Lord." This motif shows the transformation in Israel of the royal theology under the influence of the concept of blessing.

As von Rad observes, in the account of the succession to David's throne "the political conflicts are wholly rooted in personal and family affairs."[21] The reason for this is that the king, with and through his "house," is the bearer of blessing, as the Nathan oracle shows. Von Rad regards this as "one of the most conspicuous weaknesses of this history." It is possible to say this from the standpoint of a decidedly modern concept of history, but to do so is to overlook the fact that family history is continued in a different form in the kingship, and the king, with his family, is the bearer of blessing for the whole people.

Above all, the so-called messianic prophecies show with unmistakable clarity the large degree to which the king was seen as the bearer of blessing. They all are governed by the thought that the new king will bring victory and peace. In these texts this is to be accomplished not by any action in history, such as military victory, but simply by the king's birth. It is remarkable that the Messiah, who in his essence as the anointed one is the mediator of blessing, was transformed into the awaited savior figure, so that in the New Testament there was no difficulty about equating the Messiah with the *sōtēr*.

IN THE PROPHETIC BOOKS OF THE OLD TESTAMENT

In the prophetic writings, what is said about God revolves simply and clearly around God's saving actions and his corresponding judgment. It is possible to write a theology of the prophets without even mentioning the word *blessing*, and this has been done often enough. In recent research in prophecy, however, it has become clear that in the one-sided interpretation of prophecy in terms of God's deliverance and judgment important data have been overlooked. For one thing, prophets were also intercessors who were concerned with warding off threats from their fellow creatures and the world of nature. That is, they were involved in seeing to it that blessing was continued for the people. In the early period this is clearly seen in the work of Elijah

21. Ibid., p. 188.

and Elisha, and in the later period in that of Haggai. Yet there are even indications of this function in the prophets of doom. In Amos's visions (chaps. 7, 8) the prophet interceded with God for the people during a drought and a plague of locusts, and Jeremiah interceded for the people during a drought (chap. 14). The relationship of Jeremiah's activity to God's blessing his people is seen even more clearly in his letter to the exiles (29:4–7) and in his prophecy of salvation during the siege of Jerusalem (32:15). In both passages he affirms that after the future judgment has taken place God's blessing will continue.

In one of the forms of prophecy, the portrayal of salvation, God's bestowal of blessing assumes crucial importance. While the proclamation of salvation announces an event, the portrayal of salvation describes a state of well-being.[22]

The portrayal of salvation is rooted not in prophecy but in the oracle of blessing and the oracle of the seer. One example is the Judah oracle, one of the oracles about the tribes, preserved in Genesis 49 and Deuteronomy 33.

> Binding his foal to the vine
>   and his ass's colt to the choice vine,
> he washes his garments in wine
>   and his vesture in the blood of grapes.
>   (Gen. 49:11)

Another example is found in the sayings of Balaam:

> How fair are your tents, O Jacob,
>   your encampments, O Israel!
> Like valleys that stretch afar,
>   like gardens beside a river,
> like aloes that the Lord has planted,
>   like cedar trees beside the waters.
> Water shall flow from his buckets,
>   and his seed shall be in many waters.
>   (Num. 24:5–7)

The entire complex of the promises to the patriarchs consists largely of promises of blessing. What is promised is not a specific event but a state of blessedness. This is particularly clear in the promise of many descendants in such similes as "like the sand of the sea" and "like the stars of the sky."

---

22. For a discussion of this distinction see Claus Westermann, "Das Heilswort bei Deuterojesaja,"*EvTh* 24 (1964) : 355–77.

The promise of the Exodus in Exodus 3:7–8 is the proclamation of deliverance to which a promise of blessing is added: "... and to bring them up out of that land to a good and broad land, a land flowing with milk and honey." In a similar way, a promise of blessing (or a portrayal of prosperity) is added to Deutero-Isaiah's proclamation of deliverance from exile in Babylon (Isa. 54–55). There the future state of blessedness is central and the language is dominated by the vocabulary of blessing.[23]

In later prophecy, all the oracles are promises of blessing, and this carries over to apocalyptic, where the future age of prosperity is described. Since blessing and peace are so closely related, peace plays a prominent role in these promises.

> And they shall beat their swords into plowshares,
>   and their spears into pruning hooks;
> Nation shall not lift up sword against nation,
>   neither shall they learn war any more;
> but they shall sit every man under his vine
>   and under his fig tree,
> and none shall make them afraid.
>
> (Mic. 4:3b–4)

Such "messianic prophecies" as Isaiah 11 belong in this same context. In them the king of the age of prosperity is the mediator of blessing, and he brings in an era of blessing and peace.

It is thus clear that in the Old Testament, from earliest times to the latest, promises of blessing and descriptions of a state of prosperity play an important role alongside the promises of deliverance. God's promises in the Old Testament relate to his work of deliverance and to his bestowal of blessing. Each type of promise has its own form and history, and an overview must not be confined to the prophetic books. The portrayal of prosperity is found in the historical books and in the apocalyptic as well.

IN THE WRITINGS OF THE OLD TESTAMENT

In the third part of the Hebrew canon, the Writings, it is to the Psalms and the Wisdom books that we turn for information on blessing. Here too it was the discipline of the history of religion that discovered the great significance blessing had for

23. Cf. my commentary on Deutero-Isaiah in *Das Buch Jesaja*, vol. 19 of *Das Alte Testament Deutsch* (Göttingen, 1966).

worship. Because the psalms are a constituent of worship, they can yield us an overview of the role of blessing in Israel's worship.

It is a remarkable and hard-to-explain fact that in two recent treatments of worship in Israel blessing plays no role at all in one and is barely mentioned in the other.

Ernst L. Ehrlich's *Kultussymbolik im Alten Testament und im nachbiblischen Judentum,* published in 1959, gives a detailed analysis of worship procedures as found in the Old Testament and nowhere mentions blessing. The word is not even found in the index.

H.-J. Kraus's *Worship in Israel* (E. T. 1966) does not discuss blessing in the text or list it in the table of contents. The few passages given in the index under "Blessing" merely mention it. It is difficult to avoid the conclusion that the author felt blessing had no significance for the worship of Israel.

But a text like 1 Kings 8 shows otherwise. At the dedication of the newly built temple in Jerusalem, the first act performed in this sanctuary was the king's blessing of the people.[24] Then there is the solemn pronouncement of the priestly blessing in Numbers 6:22–27 and Leviticus 9:23–24. The neglect of such passages in a presentation of worship in Israel can only be the result of a prejudgment. This seems to be the same prejudgment encountered in the theologies of the Old Testament, where blessing was a priori denied all significance. On the other hand, Mowinckel takes blessing as the act that is determinative for all of worship. For example, he says: "The purpose of the cult is to secure blessing for the community and for the individual."[25] This contrast shows how much still remains to be clarified.

The temple is properly the place for bestowal of blessing (1 Kings 8). Blessing flows forth from the cultic acts in the temple upon the people and the land. Groups of pilgrims and processions go to the temple in order to obtain blessing for themselves and their families, for their cattle and their fields. If the temple should be destroyed and the worship there be ended, then the source of blessing for the land is cut off. This is shown by Solomon's prayer at the dedication of the temple (1 Kings 8), by the

24. See above, n. 19.
25. *Psalmenstudien* 5: 16.

proclamations of the prophet Haggai, and above all by the psalms of blessing and the psalms of pilgrimage (Ps. 65; 115:12–15; 128:5; 129:8; 132, etc.).[26] Not only in Israel is the worship in the temple the source of blessing for people and land; it is also the case among Israel's neighbors, in the temple worship in Canaan, in Egypt, and in Mesopotamia.[27]

The distinctiveness of Israelite worship consisted in the fact that for it history—the history of God's dealings with his people—played a decisive role. The center of Israel's worship was not some form of fertility cult that directly bestowed blessing; it was rather God's activity in history, the covenant, the commandments that grew out of the covenant, and the promises given with the covenant. This distinctive feature is seen above all in the historicizing interpretation of the annual festivals and in the transformation that turned the prayer accompanying a sacrifice into a historical confession, such as in Deuteronomy 26.

This historical center of Israel's worship did not preclude, however, the honoring of God as the source of blessing, beseeching him to bestow blessing, and the receiving of blessing. Any reconstruction of Israelite worship that stressed only its significance for the bestowal of blessing, and any reconstruction that on the contrary found in this worship only God's deeds in history, must equally be rejected as one-sided. In any case, there can be no doubt that the bestowal of blessing played a significant role in Israel's worship and that this bestowal was related to God's activity as the one who blesses.

In the priestly writings the instituting of blessing is reported, and blessing is seen as a major responsibility of the priests (Num.

26. On blessing through the psalms of pilgrimage, cf. L. J. Liebreich, "The Songs of Ascent and the Priestly Blessing," *JBL* 74 (1955) : 33–36.

27. See esp. the work of Johannes Hempel, *Die israelitischen Anschauungen von Segen und Fluch im Lichte altorientalischer Parallelen*, ZDMG, N.S. 4. In reference to the background in history of religion, Hempel supplemented this work in "Apoxysmata," *BZAW* 81 (1961) : 30–113. See also Sigmund Mowinckel, "Segen und Fluch, I: Religionsgeschichtlich," *RGG*³ 5: 1648–49; Claus Westermann, "Segen und Fluch," *EKL* 3: 916–17; G. van der Leeuw, *Phänomenologie der Religion* (1933), sec. 59: "Das Weihewort," pp. 385–86; Alfred Bertholet and E. Lehmann, *Lehrbuch der Religionsgeschichte*, 2 vols. (1925) , see in index under "Segen"; J. Scharbert, *Solidarität in Fluch und Segen*, vol. 2, pp. 72–112, "Die Solidarität des Clans bei den Nomaden der syrisch-arabischen Wüste."

6:24–26). In the structure of the Priestly Document, the first bestowal of blessing occupies a prominent position. After the desert sanctuary, the tabernacle, is set up, the first solemn sacrificial worship can take place, and at the conclusion of the sacrifice blessing is bestowed on the people, blessing valid from then on forever (Num. 9:22, 23).

A part of every gathering of the community was the blessing with which they were dismissed. This should not be thought of as merely a solemn concluding ceremony; the entire service of worship was concerned with blessing. When the priest at the conclusion pronounces Yahweh's blessing on the community, he does it so that all those who are scattering to their own homes may take with them the blessing of God that has characterized the entire sacred service. The psalms of blessing show this clearly.

Individual acts of worship are also concerned with blessing. The offering of the first fruit and grain in worship serves to promote the success of the crop, the first of which has been given to God. There were probably also blessings pronounced on individuals at specific occasions. Such Psalms as 91 and 121, which pray for the blessing of individuals, seem to point in that direction.

We can say then of Israel's worship that at its center was God's action of deliverance for his people, his mighty acts on their behalf and his covenant with them. But God's activity in blessing his people had an essential place in that worship.

Finally, a word about the relationship of wisdom to blessing. From the point of view of the proclamation of God's deeds as the central theme of the Bible, it is hard to give a clear and satisfying answer to the question of why the Wisdom literature, especially the book of Proverbs, was included in the canon. Wisdom has no connection with God's actions in history as they are summarized in the great credos. Usually the inclusion of wisdom in the canon is explained by the connection between wisdom and the fear of God, as expressed in some of the proverbs. But this connection is so limited and superficial that it can hardly be an adequate explanation.

Wisdom is rather to be seen in the context of God's bestowal of blessing. Only in this way can its inclusion in the canon be

38 BLESSING

understood. Wisdom is something that grows, and therefore it is especially to be found among the elderly. The power of growth that blessing represents has its effect on the entire person; mental powers grow along with physical strength. The maturation process involves the whole person. Wisdom can thus be seen as a result of blessing. The word that is formed by wisdom, experience, and maturity is the fruit of blessing, and therefore a collection of wisdom sayings can be included in the canon. God's power to bless is behind the wisdom sayings.[28] But also in its subject matter wisdom's closeness to blessing is seen. This originally totally secular wisdom is concerned with a victorious life, with success. The arena where wisdom's words of experience, its exhortations, and its comparisons are active is that of personal life in one's immediate circle—the home, the field, the village. These are the areas we always encounter when the effects of blessing are mentioned, especially in the patriarchal stories, in which blessing is the decisive theological concept. Even the wisdom of the court circles, which gained importance in Israel from the time of Solomon on, was not political wisdom but remained the wisdom of the home, even though this was not the royal palace.

A third connection between wisdom and blessing lies in the fact that it is not and does not claim to be specifically Israelite. It is the nature of wisdom to learn from others, and wisdom sayings can be borrowed from the Egyptians, Edomites, and other peoples. Wisdom and blessing share this universalistic aspect. Just as God gave his blessing to all living things and bestowed the power of growth on all human beings, so wisdom can increase in all men and women throughout the earth.

This connection of blessing and wisdom has great theological significance. The Old Testament speaks of a "knowledge of God" that arises only in the context of God's actions in history on behalf of Israel.[29] There is no knowledge of God apart from his

28. So also Pedersen in *Israel*, vols. 1–2, p. 198: "The blessing is the power of the soul which creates all progress; . . . therefore it is related to wisdom."
29. Hans W. Wolff, " 'Wissen um Gott' bei Hosea als Urform von Theologie," *Gesammelte Studien zum Alten Testament, ThB* 22 (1964) : 182–205.

grace manifested to his people. But the Old Testament knows a wisdom (the word *wisdom* is never used with *God*; we never find "wisdom of God") that grows out of God's power to bless, and therefore, even though it is secular wisdom, has a direct relationship to God's activity and work.

The entire book of Job is concerned with God's bestowal of blessing. The prose framework deals exclusively with this blessing—blessing in the realm of family life, as in the patriarchal narratives (Gen. 12–50), of which the prose framework of Job reminds us again and again. Blessing in this context has no relation at all to God's activity in history, and indeed it can have none because Job is not an Israelite. Of more importance, however, is the fact that in the poetic dialogues the basic question concerns God's bestowal of blessing or the withholding of that blessing. Job's friends defend the thesis that God always blesses the pious and that the withdrawal of his blessing can be understood only as God's punishment of the wicked. Job, however, will not concede that the terrible blows he has received correspond to grievous sins and faults on his part. The dramatic clash of the suffering Job's laments with the arguments advanced by his friends reveals the problem that arose because the traditional theology of blessing represented by his friends no longer corresponded to a reality in which it could not be maintained that God always blesses the pious and punishes the wicked.

In the concluding chapters of Job (chaps. 38–41) the portrayal of the reversal of events as the work of the Creator shows how creation and blessing belong together.

The relationship between God's work of deliverance and his bestowal of blessing received new expression in apocalyptic literature. Throughout the course of history the two are intertwined, but in apocalyptic they are absolutely separate. The unfolding of apocalyptic events is so intensely dramatic that there remains no room for a continuous activity of God in bestowing blessing. On the other hand, in the final state resulting from this drama, God's saving activity is no longer possible. God's work in both its aspects has achieved an absolute constancy. The pictures of salvation in the end time in apocalyptic literature present a final, immutable state of blessing, corresponding to an "eternal" destruction, from which there is no longer any deliverance.

THE HISTORY OF BLESSING IN THE OLD TESTAMENT

Following the above survey of the meaning of blessing in the various parts of the Old Testament, we turn now to a consideration of the degree to which what is said about blessing is interwoven with the history of God's people, and how rich and varied the history of blessing is.[30] In order to clarify the wider scene to which the history of blessing belongs, I will begin with the significance of the German word *segnen*, "to bless." It is derived from the Latin *signare*, "to make the sign of the cross," "to cross oneself." The expression is a part for the whole. The act of blessing consisted of an action and words, and the designation of the action came to represent the entire process. In the Christian church the bestowal of blessing was given specifically Christian meaning by the priest's making the sign of the cross, whether in worship, at baptism, or on various other occasions. This *"signare,"* however, had an effect far beyond the purely cultic activities. Members of the community crossed themselves not only during worship but in everyday activities, especially when in fear or danger or when otherwise threatened. It is well known how widely the practice prevailed in the Christian West down to the Enlightenment.

This making the sign of the cross involved calling on Christ, who died on the cross for us. But its use in times of peril shows that it does not call on the cross as a symbol of the justification of sinners. It is instead an appeal to the power of the Savior to protect, secure, defend. So also for the connection of the sign of

---

30. In this initial presentation I can give only a sketch of issues that require more detailed treatment. Three different lines of study should be followed up: first, the concept of blessing, the Hebrew root *brk*; second, the ritual of blessing both within the cult and outside it; and third, the traditional history of the formulas and oracles of blessing. For the vocabulary, see esp. A. Murtonen, op. cit.; for the formulas and oracles, see Hempel, *Die israelischen Anschauungen* . . .; Aage Bentzen, *Introduction to the Old Testament*, "Introduction to the Psalms," the section on blessing and curse; J. Scharbert, *Solidarität im Fluch und Segen*, vol. 3, chap. 4, "Familie und Nachkommen in Segenssprüchen," pp. 141–51. There are as yet no comprehensive studies of the rituals of blessing.

the cross with blessing—the sign of the cross means the imparting of blessing in the name of Christ, but the accompanying words show that blessing is seen as life power, as the presence and protection of the divine Lord. This combining of the cross, or the sign of the cross, with blessing had far-reaching consequences. We must recognize that the visible meaning of the sign of the cross and the other representations of the cross in the medieval West, with effects reaching to the present, was for ordinary men and women not primarily the *theologia crucis* that Paul set forth in his letters as the meaning of the death and resurrection of Jesus Christ, but it at least included, usually to an overwhelming extent, the idea of the God who blesses. This is shown most clearly by the crucifixes in the fields and in houses. Even when this is not always consciously realized, it is the God who bestows blessings on fields, cattle, the home, and the family, and who preserves and protects from danger, that is portrayed in the crucifix. The reason the crucifix honored in worship did not remain solely in worship but was brought into the rooms of the home and into the fields and roads is simply to express wherever it is erected the function of the God who blesses.

Seen in terms of the history of religion this means that in the Christian churches blessing has asserted itself as the power that establishes and furthers life, growth, and prosperity, and protects from harm and danger, and that it has established a remarkable connection with that which is specifically Christian—God's saving action in Christ. We can observe here the astonishing power of a religious concept and a religious procedure that did not originate in Christianity but have their roots in a very early period of human history. If the Christian faith can be termed a religion of redemption, we must see in the basic type of religion that preceded it one that was concerned not with redemption or deliverance from something but rather with the promoting, strengthening, and securing of natural existence in the world of nature. In such a religion, blessing, or something that corresponds to it, is the major concept, the major occurrence. Usually it is connected with creation; the Creator God is the God who blesses and the cultic reenactment of creation brings blessing.[31] So when in the Christian church the function of blessing became united in this manner with the symbol of redemption, this must be viewed in the context of a prehistory in which blessing enjoyed a central place in religion.

We must therefore be aware that what both Testaments say about blessing preserves the memory of a procedure that was once central to religion. It is then clear that what the Bible says about blessing involves not something that still survives somehow on the periphery of the biblical message but something that was once of all-encompassing significance for religion. It also becomes clear that on one hand blessing can never be fully "Christianized" (in everything said about blessing a certain heritage is still there), and on the other hand any attempt to remove blessing from Christian speech and action (by saying, for example, that it is a kind of petition) is futile.

THE INSTITUTION OF THE PRIESTLY BLESSING

I will begin with the final stage, which we find in the instituting of the priestly blessing as it is given in the priestly document in Numbers 6:22–27:

> The Lord said to Moses, "Say to Aaron and his sons, Thus you shall bless the people of Israel: you shall say to them,
>> The Lord bless you and keep you:
>> The Lord make his face to shine upon you, and be gracious to you:
>> The Lord lift up his countenance upon you, and give you peace.
> So shall they put my name upon the people of Israel, and I will bless them."[32]

---

31. The connection between creation and blessing is especially clear and impressive in Sumerian mythology. See N. S. Kramer, *Sumerian Mythology* (1944) and my comments in the introduction to the primeval history in *Genesis, Biblischer Kommentar,* vol. 1, esp. pp. 79–80; see also Mowinckel, *Religion und Kultus* (1953) , p. 26–27.

32. Even this apparently typical Israelite formulation of the blessing belongs to a traditional context of blessing in worship that extends far beyond Israel. An example from Jastrow's *Die Religion Babyloniens and Assyriens* 1: 343:

> May the word of Ea shine forth!
> May Damkina guide rightly!
> O Marduk, firstborn son of Abyss:
> lustre and purification belong to thee!

This presupposes the fixed institution of the cult, the sanctuary, the legitimate priesthood ("Aaron and his sons"), and the firm connection of this cultic institution with the history of God's deeds on behalf of Israel (in the figure of Moses). This is the institution of the blessing of the community by the priest, which we find in several psalms and other passages (e.g., Ps. 118:26b: "We bless you from the house of the Lord") and which actually continued essentially unaltered throughout the history of the worship of ancient Israel from its origins on through the postexilic temple and synagogue worship into Christian worship, where it has maintained its place to the present day. The distinctive features that can be identified in this origin are the following:

(a) The real subject of the action, the one who acts through the activity of the priest, is God.

(b) The act of blessing includes both word and rite.

(c) Blessing involves God's friendly approach to those who will receive him. Its meaning is discovered in the contexts that present God's actions of bestowing blessing.

(d) The appropriate place for the blessing is at the end of worship when the community is dismissed. The blessing is to go with those who receive it, out into their life outside the times of worship.

None of the basic features of this bestowal of blessing had altered from the time it was instituted, although the way they were interpreted remained open. The final stage seen here was

---

Jastrow quoted from Hylmö an even closer parallel to Num. 6:

> Ea rejoice over thee!
> Damkina, the queen of the ocean,
> illumine thee by her face!
> Marduk, the prince of the gods,
> raise up thy head!

This can be compared to the form of the Aarònic blessing found at Qumran in the *Manual of Discipline.*

> May he bless thee with every good
> and keep thee from every evil:
> and illumine thy heart with life-giving wisdom
> and favour thee with eternal knowledge
> and lift up His face of mercy
> toward thee for thine eternal peace!

See also Theodorus C. Vriezen, *Ned. TTs,* 1952, p. 101.

preceded by a long, complex history. Two of the above features remained the same through all stages of this history, as far as the bestowal of blessing is concerned. That is to say, they extend from the oldest textual evidence to the final stage. One is the connection of word and rite; the other is the particular place of blessing at the time of dismissal. Significant changes can be seen in the subject and the object of the blessing.[33]

The psalms presuppose the institution of priestly blessing, and it is reflected in many of them that speak of the bestowal and receipt of blessing.[34] The priests bless the community (Ps. 115: 14–15; 118:26; 129:8; 134:3) or an individual (91; 121). From the sanctuary blessing is bestowed on the community (118:26; 24:5; 128:5). The congregation asks God to bless it (Ps. 67:1). Blessing is promised to those who fear God (Ps. 24:5; 128:4). God, as creator, is the one who blesses (Ps. 115:15–16; 121:2; 128; 134:3).

The structure of the Priestly Document reveals the significance of blessing for theology and for worship. The priestly blessing is not introduced to or made operational in worship in Numbers 6:22–27; this was done earlier at the end of the series of events that follow the appearance of God on Mount Sinai (Exod. 19:1–2a; 24:15b–18). In the theophany at Sinai, Moses receives the commission to build the "Tent of Meeting" (Exod. 25:1ff.). This is detailed in Exodus 25–31, and the carrying out of the commission is recounted in chapters 35–40. Then follow the laws for sacrifices (Lev. 1–7) and the induction of Levi and his sons into the priestly office (Lev. 8). This sequence reaches its goal in the first service of worship and sacrifice (Lev. 9), at the end of which stands the blessing (Lev. 9:22–23). This first offering of sacrifice, which concludes with the blessing, is then authenticated or con-

33. Much more could be said in regard to the institution of the priestly blessing, but no preliminary work has been done here. In Roland de Vaux's great work, *Ancient Israel: Its Life and Institutions* (New York: McGraw-Hill, 1961), the second part of which deals in detail with the cultic institutions, there is no discussion of the institution of blessing. In the entire work blessing is mentioned only a single time.

To call the cultic institution of blessing the final stage has validity only in terms of a general sketch. The Qumran documents, for example, show that the development continued. See M. R. Lehmann, *RQ* 3 (1961): 120.

34. See Mowinckel, *Psalmenstudien* 5: 33–57, "Segenspsalmen"; and Hermann Gunkel and Joachim Begrich, *Einleitung in die Psalmen* (1933), pp. 293–309.

firmed by the appearing of God's glory (Lev. 9:23b). In this way the validity of the blessing as the conclusion of worship is confirmed permanently.

BLESSING IN DEUTERONOMY

What is said about blessing in Deuteronomy can be distinguished from the institutional nature of blessing in Numbers 6 and identified as a distinct stage in the development.[35] Certain features are prominent:

(a) The recipient of the blessing is the people of Israel. At the initiation of the priestly blessing in Numbers 6 it is also Israel that is blessed, but there all the emphasis is on Israel's being assembled at the sanctuary for worship. Deuteronomy stresses that God gives his blessing to all the nation in every area of its life, without picturing it as the community gathered for worship. The distinction can be clearly seen if Numbers 6 and the passage in Deuteronomy 11 are read together; as the people enter the land they are to place blessing and curse on two mountains, that is, on the land. "And when the Lord your God brings you into the land which you are entering to take possession of it, you shall set the blessing on Mount Gerizim and the curse on Mount Ebal" (Deut. 11:29). This act was intended to document the fact that God's promise to give Israel the land has now been fulfilled and that God's blessing on the land into which he has led them is now in effect (cf. Josh. 5:11–12). The blessing intended for Israel is here brought into close connection with the blessing of the land. It is the people that have settled down in the land who now receive God's blessing.

(b) The blessing given to the Israelites in their land is manifested essentially in the produce of the land. Blessing as formulated in Numbers 6 sounds primarily "spiritual" (the grace of God, God's face, shines upon them), but the blessing which Deuteronomy speaks of is as secular, as this-worldly, as can be imagined. "He will love you, bless you, and multiply you; he

---

35. See Gerhard von Rad, *Das Gottesvolk im Deuteronomium, BWANT* 17 (1929) ; and, more recently, J. G. Plöger, *Literarkritische, formgeschichtliche und stilkritische Untersuchungen zum Deuteronomium, BBB* 26 (1967) .

will also bless the fruit of your body and the fruit of your ground, your grain and your wine and your oil, the increase of your cattle and the young of your flock, in the land which he swore to your fathers to give you" (Deut. 7:13; cf. 28:3–6).

Here blessing is the power of growth—of fertility, of prosperity as that power expresses itself in a healthy people in a fertile land. Here as elsewhere it is the threefold fertility of body, field, and cattle. This is how blessing was understood by the people of Israel after they became settled in Canaan as farmers. God's gracious approach to the people as it is expressed through blessing works itself out essentially in the power of fertility, which means life. Gerhard von Rad pointed out the strikingly worldly character of the understanding of blessing in Deuteronomy:

> It seems paradoxical, but Israel was perhaps never more pious in its receiving gifts directly from God's hands than it was in Deuteronomy in receiving these material things. Neither in the times before Deuteronomy nor in subsequent periods do we find this simple, unselfconscious willingness to accept earthly gifts, not as the rewards of spiritual qualities, but unmerited, accepted from God simply for their own sake. From this we are to understand that Yahweh's blessing, which brings about the whole physical life of God's people, is the gift of salvation par excellence.[36]

(c) The celebration of Yahweh in Deuteronomy in this vivid manner as the bestower of blessing was the result of a tremendous struggle. For Deuteronomy itself the struggle had long been won. We find it in the prophets, especially Hosea and Elijah. At issue was whether the gods of the land, the Baals, remained the source of fertility or whether Yahweh, the God who rescued and led the group of wanderers, could become the source of fertility as well. This was one of the hardest spiritual contests in the entire history of Israel, and it decided the question of where the source of the power of blessing was to be sought. The form of Israel's faith that has come down to us rests to a large extent on the outcome of this struggle to show

36. *Das Gottesvolk im Deuteronomium* (1929), p. 42.

that Yahweh was also to be acclaimed and honored as the source of blessing. This shows that any reduction of Israel's faith to God's acts in history is a basic misinterpretation of that faith. The confession of Yahweh as Israel's God who rescued his people from Egypt is recited in Deuteronomy 26 when the first-fruits are offered. Israel's deliverer has become the bestower of blessing. It is from his hand that the gifts of the land are received.

(d) Deuteronomy constantly refers to God's promises to the patriarchs (6:10; 8:1; and many other passages). This is the land that God "swore to your fathers, to Abraham, to Isaac, and to Jacob, to give you" (6:10). The promise of the land is part of the context of promises of blessing, and we find here the transition from an earlier to a later stage of what is said about blessing. In the patriarchal narratives the family or clan is the recipient of blessing—a man is blessed together with his "house." But when the descendants of the patriarchs are promised possession of the land of Canaan, this means the transition to the nation as the recipient. It is clear that with this change much must be altered when speaking about blessing. Since the power of blessing operates in all aspects of existence, the blessing that rests on family or clan must differ from that of a nation even though many features remain the same.

In Deuteronomy this change is presupposed as having taken place much earlier. It is assumed without question that the recipient of blessing is the nation. There are, however, two bodies of material in the Old Testament in which this transition is still in progress—the Yahwist document and the Balaam narrative, with its oracles (see below). In both instances we can observe the development of the concept of blessing out of the prehistoric life of the clan into the historical life of the nation. What Deuteronomy says about blessing stands then between an earlier stage at which blessing belonged to the realm of family life where a man was blessed with and in his clan, and a later stage when blessing was an institution within worship and the recipient was the community assembled for worship.

(e) Blessing in Deuteronomy can be distinguished from the

earlier, patriarchal stage by a specific, all-pervading characteristic. Blessing is always spoken of as conditional; it depends on the obedience of God's people (Deut. 7:12–13):

> And because you hearken to these ordinances, and keep and do them, the Lord your God will keep with you the covenant and the steadfast love which he swore to your fathers to keep; he will love you, bless you, and multiply you; he will also bless the fruit of your body and the fruit of your ground, your grain and your wine and your oil, the increase of your cattle and the young of your flock, in the land which he swore to your fathers to give you.

This dependence of blessing on the people's obedience is stressed throughout the book and is of great significance for the concept of blessing. It shows the connection of blessing with history. Blessing has become a component of the covenant between God and the people; as the above quotation shows, God keeps his covenant with Israel by blessing them, but this requires that the nation also keep the covenant.[37] We must remember that this merging of blessing with the covenant signified a far-reaching transformation of the concept of blessing and the way it was understood at an earlier stage. At the earlier stage blessing was unconditional. When a person was blessed the blessing could not be withdrawn. In Deuteronomy, however, it is characteristic of the concept of blessing that by being connected with the covenant it is tied to the obedience of the people. As a result, blessing is necessarily subject to possible limits. When the people are commanded as they enter the land (Deut. 11:29) not simply to place blessing on the land but to place blessing on Mount Gerizim and curse on Mount Ebal, a limitation of God's granting of blessing is depicted. Because blessing is tied to the people's obedience, the curse henceforth stands side by side with blessing as a possibility. These two possibilities confronting Israel are developed in chapters 27 and 28. The instruction mentioned above is repeated (27:11–13), and in 28:1ff. and 28:15ff. the people are confronted

---

37. There is need for specific research into the relation of blessing to the "covenant formula," the formula's role and its function in treaties, and the influence of this function on the concept of blessing. In relation to Deuteronomy, see B. K. Baltzer, *Das Bundesformular* (1960), pp. 40–47 (*The Covenant Formulary* [Philadelphia: Fortress Press, 1971]) and n. 44 below.

in deadly earnest with the choice that will determine their future. The curse that will result from disobedience is described in terrifying terms unlike anything else in the Bible (28:15–68). It signifies disaster, terror, and destruction.

Deuteronomy is thus particularly important for the development of blessing because here we find the connection between the theology of blessing and that of deliverance. By the transformation of blessing into something conditional, God's activity in granting blessing becomes limited by the curse that enters where Israel ceases to be obedient. This curse is identical with the judgment of God proclaimed by the prophets. The polarity of blessing and curse is here linked to the polarity of deliverance and judgment, although these two pairs of contrasts originally had nothing to do with each other. Deuteronomy therefore reveals a clear and close connection between a theology whose center is blessing and one whose center is deliverance. This connection can be seen even in the choice of language. Many of the expressions in the great chapter of curses, Deuteronomy 28, are known to us from the prophetic announcements of judgment.

It should also be noted that Deuteronomy, as it has come down to us, is the product of a long and complicated history of transmission. The striking juxtaposition of passages that speak of blessing as a gift to be received in tranquil thankfulness, and others that speak of the threat to blessing posed so powerfully by the curse, is in part to be explained as successive stages, because parts of Deuteronomy—for example, parts of chapter 28—date from the period of the Exile.

BLESSING IN THE YAHWIST SOURCE AND THE BALAAM PERICOPE

The Yahwist document and the Balaam pericope represent the next earlier stage in the presentation of blessing in the Old Testament. In both bodies of material the originally nonhistorical or prehistorical concept of blessing is brought into union with history. That is, blessing becomes a constituent part of the history of God's dealings with his people.

(a) In the Balaam pericope, Numbers 22–24, we read that Balak, king of Moab, fearing an attack by the Israelites, sends for the seer Balaam of Pethor on the Euphrates, "for I know that he

whom you bless is blessed, and he whom you curse is cursed"
(22:6). Balaam accedes to the request, but Yahweh, God of Israel,
commands him not to curse them but to bless. "You shall not
curse the people, for they are blessed" (22:12b). Balaam blesses
Israel in his prophetic oracles, in which he promises them future
salvation.

This story presupposes the existence of gifted individuals who
have the power to bless and to curse. This gift of uttering power-
laden words does not depend on their belonging to any nation
or religion, and the power possessed by these individuals can be
placed at the disposal of others for pay. Here we see a pre-Israelite
concept that is encountered in many places around the world, the
concept of the experiencing of a powerful utterance spoken by a
properly endowed person with results that can be beneficial or
harmful.[38] In the Balaam stories it is explicitly recognized that
there is a connection between God's activity directed toward the
blessing of Israel, and this generally known and widespread phenomenon of the history of religion where the spoken word is
laden with power. This fact must not be ignored. Israel knew
that God's power to bestow the blessings by which they lived
derived from and was a part of a phenomenon that had existed
before Israel and continued outside Israel. The first blessing that
Israel received on their way to the Promised Land came by means
of a non-Israelite, a foreigner who served a foreign god. Nonetheless, in this one special case, that non-Israelite responded to the
irresistible word of Israel's God and, following his command,
blessed rather than cursed Israel.

The narrative explains how it came to pass that Yahweh the
God of Israel became master of this power to bless—a power that
existed and was recognized previously—and how this power was
made to serve the history of Israel's dealings with their God, thus
rendering all possibilities of a power-laden word outside Israel
both powerless and meaningless. The reason this story unfolds
immediately before the entry into the Promised Land is that
Yahweh, who had until then been the God who rescues and
guides, became, with the occupation of the land, also the God
who blesses.

38. See the above citations of literature in history of religion that deals with
blessing.

The significance of this story for the understanding of blessing in the Old Testament lies in the fact that here the biblical concept of blessing is brought into relation to manifestation of a power-filled word in the world outside the Bible.[39]

(b) The Yahwist, who composed his great work in the days of David or Solomon, brought together in it three major cycles of tradition that had formerly been independent of each other: the history of the people, the patriarchal narratives, and the primeval history. His great contribution consisted in bringing together into a unified whole three cycles that once had been separate and each of which had its own theology or represented its own type of religion, thus creating a great historical work that covered three epochs. In the stories of the patriarchs as the Yahwist found them, the distinctive concept for the dealings of God with man was blessing. This concept antedated history or was nonhistorical, because what occurs in these stories is prior to history and concerns the family or clan. The essential events are events in family life—birth, marriage, and death. Blessing was related to them in that they arose out of the power given in blessing. The continuity of the effect of blessing is shown by the genealogies, the outlines of family history. The Yahwist then combined this prehistoric view of blessing with history by connecting blessing to God's promise, and thereby blessing became a component of history.

The Yahwist begins the patriarchal stories with God's command to Abraham to leave his homeland. In Genesis 12:1–3 this command is connected with blessing:

> Now the Lord said to Abram, "Go from your country and your kindred and your father's house to the land that I will show you. And I will make you a great nation, and I will bless you, and make your name great, so that you will be a blessing. I will bless those who bless you, and him who curses you I will curse; and by you all the families of the earth shall bless themselves."

In this prologue to the patriarchal narratives the two basic motifs are introduced: the migration of the patriarchs and the

---

39. On Balaam and the oracles, see the following lexicon articles: *RGG*[3] (Rolfe Rendtdorff), *BHH* (L. M. Pakozdy), and *IDB* (R. F. Johnson), and the bibliography in *IDB*. See also D. Vetter, "Untersuchungen zum Seherspruch," unpublished Heidelberg dissertation (1962).

hints of their goal. These motifs form a connection with the history of the nation in that the command to set out corresponds to the same motif at the opening of the book of Exodus, and the goal here to the goal there. The promise of blessing spans the distance between the start of the migration and the envisioned goal. In this way the concept of blessing that the Yahwist took up is thoroughly altered. Formerly it was recounted how a father, before his death, blessed his son; when the act of blessing was concluded the son was blessed. So what is meant by blessing is not something that can be promised. The Yahwist gave blessing the aspect of something future and thus made it the object of Yahweh's promise. Blessing became a constituent part of history. The cycle of Abraham stories does not begin with Abraham receiving God's blessing and then this blessing coming to pass in what befalls Abraham. Rather, Abraham at the outset receives the command to go forth, and the blessing that is connected with this is not simply there, but it is seen in prospect, so that it comes to pass in the history that begins with Abraham and continues not just throughout his lifetime but on after his death. Compared with the idea of blessing in the older patriarchal narratives, this is a totally new concept—blessing has been incorporated into history. This blessing that is transformed into promise is found not only in 12:1-3 but also in many other passages throughout the patriarchal history where God's blessing is promised to the patriarchs.

A further change took place with this transformation of blessing into something historical. In the older patriarchal stories, blessing is dependent on an action. Since blessing resembles a transfer of power, some action or gesture is a necessary part of it. Even when the power is seen as divine, or at least in some sense transcendent, the transfer can take place only in some sort of action. This connection between word and action disappears when God is the one who blesses, or where God promises blessing. This means that an extensive transformation of the old concept of blessing took place, in that in the transfer to Yahweh, Israel's God, of all power to bless, the action was separated from blessing, and blessing as an action of God was set free from any concrete act of transmittal, any visible gesture of contact. God's blessing is present only in its results as its power is seen at work in the life of the individual or the nation. We may call this a theologizing of blessing, and we must regard this transformation of a bestowal of power through an act accessible to our senses into an action ascribed to the invisible God, recognizable only in its effects, as one of the most theologically significant innovations of the early history of Israel.[40]

If we compare the way in which the Yahwist incorporated the concept of blessing into the ancient Israelite theology of history and the way this was done in the Balaam pericope, we discover a significant difference alongside the elements they have in common. The Balaam pericope is rooted in a well-known phenomenon that is widespread in the history of religions, the transfer of power through the words of an especially endowed person. The Yahwist draws on the concept of the transfer of power through a blessing that passes from father to child. We can thus assume that here we find two phenomena which in terms of the history of religion can be clearly distinguished but are closely related, and which in the course of history merged into the biblical concept of blessing.

BLESSING IN THE PATRIARCHAL NARRATIVES

This brings us to the earliest stage of the history of blessing that can be found in the Old Testament. In the preceding discus-

---

40. I will cite only the most recent of the many studies of the theology of the Yahwist: Hans W. Wolff, "Das Kerygma des Jahwisten," *EvTh* 24 (1964): 73–98 (reprinted in *Gesammelte Studien*, pp. 345–73). Wolff lists and discusses the most important literature. He pays particular attention to Gen. 12:1–4a (pp. 351ff.). In response to the question of the tradition that stands behind this passage he says: "Only in terms of the traditional material of promise is the main theme of the passage, the five variations of the word 'blessing,' understandable. It was not invented by the Yahwist, but is at home in the promise of a son or of prosperity." Wolff treats briefly the basic meaning of the word and then explains the way in which the Yahwist interpreted the tradition: "In the old clan structure blessing was understood as a powerful word that had immediate effect, but here (in connection with the promise of countless posterity) it is a promise directed to the future. 'Blessing' is a key word of the whole history of Israel from Abraham's departure from Ur to the empire of David. . . . The old word teaches us to understand the new history." Wolff's view is along the same line as the explanation given here, even though Wolff does not emphasize the fact that a change from the originally nonhistorical concept to a historical one had already occurred in the transformation of blessing into the promise of blessing. On this transformation of the concept of blessing by the Yahwist, see my articles on blessing in *EKL* and *BHH*.

sion we have assumed that it is necessary to distinguish in Genesis 12–50 between the form that the Yahwist gave to these stories that had come to him and the stories themselves, insofar as they reach back to an earlier age. The differences between these two strands of tradition is seen with particular clarity in what they say about blessing. We may assume that the Yahwist's transformation of the concept of blessing is centuries later than the material in the old stories. But even there the material is not all of one piece. We encounter traces of a rich and varied development of blessing in prehistoric times in the realm of the clan. Only a few features of this development can be indicated here.

(a) The old concept of blessing is seen most clearly in Genesis 27, where we are told that Jacob obtained his father Isaac's blessing by deceit.[41] The essential elements of this story are as follows:

(1) The blessing is the power of life handed on from father to son. The word has here its original meaning of the power of fertility and prosperity.[42] This power affects not only the one blessed but also his possessions, in this case especially his cattle.

(2) The father has only *one* blessing to bestow. This must indicate an earlier understanding of blessing, because in another passage in the patriarchal narratives, the blessing of Jacob's sons, there is nothing to hinder his blessing all twelve sons.

(3) Blessing cannot be recalled, and it works unconditionally. This feature plays a significant role in the story. If blessing is once bestowed, this action cannot be annulled.

(4) The time when blessing is bestowed is when the father awaits his death.

(5) The bestowal of blessing, or its transfer to the son, follows a clearly identifiable ritual, including a series of actions and the words of blessing. The story is structured after the order of the ritual.

(6) Blessing here still has a pretheological character. In the ritual and in the words of blessing God is not mentioned, and it

---

41. So also Hempel, *Die israelischen Anschauungen*, ZDMG, N.S. 4, p. 23.
42. This basic meaning, which was developed especially in Johannes Pedersen's work, has recently been confirmed in A. Murtonen and H. Mowvley, "The Concept and Content of 'Blessing' in the Old Testament," *The Bible Translator* 16 (1965) : 74–80.

is not even said that, in the blessing Isaac bestows, God is the one who blesses. Nor is there anyone who mediates the blessing: the father bestows it. So the ritual here is also precultic.

(b) Another typical process of blessing is recounted in the courting of Rebecca. Her brothers send her away from the clan and her homeland with the blessing "Our sister, be the mother of thousands of ten thousands; and may your descendants possess the gate of those who hate them!" (Gen. 24:60). We may assume that such a parting blessing was a fixed custom at the departure of a member of the clan and that it took various forms. There is probably a particular reason that it is the brothers who pronounce the blessing here. The addition of a promise of victory to that of blessing probably represents a later stage. This may be compared with Genesis 9:25–27.

(c) In the cycle of stories about Jacob and Esau, the concept of blessing shows considerable reflection on its meaning and is highly developed in its use. Although the cycle of Abraham stories is more deeply impregnated with the promise of blessing, in the stories of Jacob and Esau the narrator is especially concerned with the procedure of blessing and its consequences.[43]

(d) Quite different from the other passages is Genesis 32, where a blessing is won in combat. We can only observe that here there is a motif that is foreign to the other stories and that must go back to a very early time. Genesis 32 may contain echoes of a concept that is found outside the Old Testament, a mythological concept according to which a god or a divine being controls the power of blessing and, under certain circumstances, can communicate it even to a human being—but only in a bodily encounter, whether that is a combat as here in Genesis 32 or some other type of physical contact.

(e) An intermediate stage between the blessing in the family, as depicted in the patriarchal narratives, and the blessing that God bestows on his people, is the blessing of the tribe, that is, the blessing promised a single tribe. This blessing is found in two collections, Genesis 49 and Deuteronomy 33 (as well as in certain

---

43. See Claus Westermann, "Arten der Erzählung in der Genesis," in *Gesammelte Studien,* pp. 9–91, especially the fifth section, the Jacob-Esau cycle (pp. 74–82) , where I have developed this more fully.

scattered passages). The tribal blessings collected in these chapters were afterward ascribed to Jacob and Moses. The oracles originated separately and in themselves have nothing to do with blessing, but there is a connection between the pronouncement of blessing and the sayings concerning the tribes, as can be seen in such passages as Genesis 24:60 and in the sayings about Shem, Ham, and Japhet in Genesis 9:25–27. We know very little, however, of the intermediate stages of blessing and oracles of blessing in the individual tribes.[44]

Concluding Comments on Blessing in the Patriarchal Narratives

The difference between the way the Yahwist understood blessing and the ideas in the old narratives is so unmistakable and so great that we can with certainty assign the concept of blessing that is found, for example, in the story in Genesis 27, to the period of the patriarchs before the exodus from Egypt and before the tribes came together. That is to say, it belongs to the time before Yahweh encountered Israel.

Certain features indicate the remnants of a magical concept of blessing. Blessing is a transfer of power that involves physical contact. The act of blessing requires that the one bestowing blessing be strengthened by eating special food. The power is exhausted in a single act of blessing; Jacob receives only one blessing. The blessing cannot be canceled, and it works unconditionally. The act of blessing precedes both theology and cultic ritual; God is not mentioned in it. All these features remind us of magical procedures that are well known from the history of religion.[45]

---

44. The question should be raised as to whether there is a connection between the blessings on the tribes, which according to Gen. 49 and Deut. 33 must have played a major role in early times, and the blessing in the later worship of Israel, first of all in the gatherings of the tribes under the covenant and its institutions. A similar surmise is made by W. J. Harrelson in "Blessings and Cursings," *IDB* 1: 447: "Within the confederacy of the twelve tribes of Israel prior to the establishment of the monarchy, blessings and cursings were probably a regular part of the festival of covenant renewal (Josh. 24; cf. Deut. 11:26–32; 27–29) ."

45. Special reference should be made to the words of Mowinckel in his *Psalmenstudien* and to Hempel, *Die israelischen Anschauungen*, "Die Verwurzelung im Magischen," pp. 22ff.

The following observations may be made:

(1) There is no point in denying or explaining away the magical characteristics that cling to this early stage of blessing. They are there. The only question is how they are to be evaluated.

(2) We belong to a culture in which magic and the magical are automatically regarded negatively. Magic is something inferior, primitive, stupid, evil (but with all that, it is somewhat uncanny). This judgment is based primarily on evolutionary belief and a scale of values that goes with it. Even though this belief has long been abandoned, the scale of values has remained. Only in the most recent stage of the scientific study of religion and in ethnology has a basic alteration taken place.[46] In this newer approach, magic is placed on the same level as religion and even science, as one of the possible ways for man to control reality, or to put it differently, one of the possible ways to encounter powers and forces that are superior to man and that can be at his disposal. To belittle magic no longer makes sense, and such an attitude can only be ascribed to a lack of knowledge or to preconceptions.

(3) We must then recognize that the history of blessing in the Bible reaches back to an early stage in which the actions connected with the bestowal of blessing still had magical features. It must be admitted that these traces of magic were not eradicated from these old stories as they were handed down, but were preserved. If the Yahwist exhibits a concept of blessing that is fundamentally different and understands it in a manner basically different from the ideas found in the old narratives, and yet does not purge these narratives of the magical traits connected with blessing, we must assume that he recognized in this pre-Yahwistic, pretheological understanding of blessing some positive significance. The point may cautiously be expressed in the following manner. The Yahwist, the theologian of the age of David or Solomon, felt it was important for his generation and subsequent generations to know that blessing had this origin and this pre-

46. I would mention above all G. van der Leeuw, *Phänomenologie der Religion* (1948), and Claude Lévi-Strauss, *Structural Anthropology* (New York: Doubleday, 1967), ch. 3, "Magic and Religion."

history. We should take a similar position. We should, first of all, without making any value judgments, recognize that blessing, a component of our present theological vocabulary and our present worship, goes back in its prehistory not merely into the stage of primitive religion but also into the realm of magic.

(4) In the theology of the Yahwist, the magical nature of blessing was modified when blessing became a historical concept connected with God's promise, and thus a component of the history of Yahweh's dealings with his people. In the Deuteronomic theology this theologizing of blessing was strengthened by the connection of blessing with the covenant, and in this way it became conditional. The magical features of blessing were entirely eliminated, and it became possible to fully incorporate blessing into the Yahweh faith. The continued transmission of the older tradition, however, left traces that could not be combined with this faith on the same plane.

(5) We are then able to identify in the history of blessing in the Old Testament two tendencies that together are determinative for this history. The first is the tendency to modify the existing understanding of blessing by the theological conceptions of the present, to approach it differently, and to understand it in a basically new way. The second is the tendency to retain the traditional understanding of blessing that cannot be represented in the standard theology and to continue to transmit it. We see here the sense of history that exerted such strong influence on the thought of ancient Israel and on the theology of the Old Testament. The contemporary theological conception was never absolutized, and the earlier concepts that had been "superseded" were never silenced but were allowed to continue to speak in the ongoing tradition and thus to be heard by posterity.

(6) The Priestly Document provides another impressive example of this basic orientation which the concept of blessing had to history. The same Priestly Document that in Numbers 6 contains the institution of the priestly blessing, which as the latest stage in the history of blessing in the Old Testament was the starting point for our study, gives the concept of blessing in Genesis 1 a totally different meaning from that which it had in Numbers 6. In Numbers 6, the Priestly Document presents a

concept of blessing that is strictly defined by the sacral and is clearly confined to the practices of the cultic worship in Jerusalem. In Genesis 1, however, the concept of blessing has the widest meaning that it has anywhere in the Bible. The creator blesses what he has created—all mankind and all living creatures (Gen. 1:22, 28). And when in addition in Genesis 2:3 the seventh day is not only declared holy but also blessed and sanctified, the same powerful scope of God's blessing is depicted. The blessing bestowed in worship, even when it is tied to sacral acts and limited to the circle of those gathered there, is intended in reality for the whole of mankind. And the blessing that is bestowed on the community that has gathered for worship is thought of as applying to the whole human race, indeed to all living beings, just as blessing in its original sense meant the power of life. In this way the priestly theology, reaching as it does the entire span from Genesis 1 to Numbers 6, includes the entire history of blessing with all its possibilities.

BLESSING AND GREETING IN THE OLD TESTAMENT

It is not possible to portray the history of blessing in the Old Testament without considering the close connection that the greeting had with blessing.[47] Three factors unite the greeting with blessing. (a) An important occasion for blessing is leave-taking. In this situation blessing and greeting come together. The opposite situation of meeting someone requires another sort of greeting. (b) Both greeting and blessing involve words and actions. Even though in a greeting the action may be reduced to a gesture, their relationship is so firm that it has endured through the centuries to the present day. (c) They have in common that

47. In the works cited above, the monographs and lexicon articles generally speak of the greeting in the context of blessing; e.g., Johannes Hempel, Friedrich Horst, J. Scharbert, Walter J. Harrelson. But only Johannes Pedersen examined the meaning of this connection more closely. The real meaning of the greeting in the Old Testament is seen only here. Pedersen said in part: "Human intercourse is impossible without blessing. . . . When people meet, they bless each other. . . . For peoples like Israel the greeting is a formality that entails a deep reality, as all other forms with primitive peoples. He who has traveled in the desert knows what it means to meet a man who does not salute, but pulls his kerchief down over his face and passes on. . . . The greeting is the establishment or confirmation of psychic communion. Therefore it is tantamount to a blessing" (*Israel,* p. 202).

a pretheological and a precultic origin is still recognizable in both. Yes, in the greeting its pretheological, secular character has continued through a long history. It cannot be disputed that the greeting, in all its forms, such as congratulating, wishing a happy birthday, or expressing good wishes at major festivals, had its origin in a magical understanding of existence. The function of the greeting in our enlightened, secularized world still retains a component of magical thought and practice, though highly sublimated. In terms of our scientific understanding of the world and humanity, a greeting has no meaning at all. Yet we all know that if greetings disappeared a part of our humanity would disappear with them. (d) Greeting and blessing have a large part of their vocabulary in common. Above all, the word *peace* that is so important in greetings (*shālōm, eirēnē, salus, Heil*) was originally used in bestowing blessing.

The relationship of greeting to blessing can be seen in many passages of the Old Testament and in many different expressions. Often they are identical, as in the beautiful and profound episode in Genesis 47:7–10, where Joseph presents his father to Pharaoh and Jacob bestows his blessing on the king. Here in the greeting, blessing, in the full sense of the term, occurs. The scene has a dignity that makes it understandable without any explanation of why the poor nomadic herdsman is able to bless the powerful Pharaoh and why that blessing has power.[48] Many other scenes could be added to this one.

In the New Testament as well as the Old, the greeting has remarkable vitality. In contrast to our modern world, greetings had not yet become strictly formalized phenomena on the periphery of human society but had a central significance for the common life of human beings. The words that people use to greet one another in the Bible are much less formal, show much more variety, and mean what they say. This is the reason that in many biblical narratives the greetings have essential meaning for the action. When Jonathan says to David, who has to flee for safety, "Go in peace" (1 Sam. 20:42), this parting word gives to the one

48. See ibid., p. 203: "Also the lesser people may, according to their humble means, bless the great. Thus they confirm the blessing which the great naturally possess, and thus they contribute to its increase (Job 31:20)."

who is now insecure a pledge of peace on which he can rely. In the Joseph story, when the brothers do not give any greeting to Joseph, whom their father has sent to them, the rift in the family relationship is clearly expressed (Gen. 37:4). In the portrayal of Jehu's revolt (2 Kings 9), the climax of the drama is skillfully intensified in the exchange of questions about what is happening, which is a sort of exchange of greetings. When we turn to the New Testament, in Luke 1–2 greetings are an essential component of the narrative, especially the greeting of the angel to Mary. Medieval paintings often show the closeness of greeting to blessing by picturing the angel as giving a blessing.

It is not possible here to describe the variety, the deep significance, and the value of greeting in the Old Testament; it must suffice to stress the passages where it is involved with blessing and its relation to blessing.

I said above that the establishment of blessing as a cultic institution represented the final stage of the history of blessing in the Old Testament. That statement must now be supplemented and to some extent corrected. The earlier stages were not simply eliminated. Two lines that go back to the earliest stage continued outside the main line but became part of the cultic, institutional blessing. The blessing of children by their parents continued to be a part of family life from generation to generation. We see it especially in the book of Tobit, which reminds us in the other ways too of the patriarchal narratives. The blessing that was identical with a greeting followed an independent course as the greeting developed and took on a highly significant role in the community. The theological interpretation of blessing worked in such a way that the greeting also came to have a close connection with the activity of God. We find this connection in everyday greetings from New Testament times through the Middle Ages, and in modern times there are such greetings as the German *"Grüss Gott!"* and the Israeli greeting of *"Shālōm."* More important, however, is the fact that the blessing imparted in worship maintained its connection with ordinary greetings, regardless of the vocabulary used. In the same way that God's blessing was bestowed on the community gathered for worship in the temple, this giving and receiving of blessing continued to be expressed in the exchange of ordinary greetings. Whenever a father sent his son off on a long and dangerous journey with a blessing (Tobit 5:16), he was passing on the blessing received in the service of worship. The Old Testament could not speak as it does of blessing and the effects of God's blessing if this passing on of blessing in greetings, this distribution of blessing, were not a reality. The pronouncing of a blessing at mealtime should be mentioned here as well as another way in which blessing is carried from worship into daily life. This close, indissoluble connection between a rite observed in worship—the imparting of blessing to the community —and an ordinary form of the community's life together is of great significance for the twofold commission that Jesus gives to his disciples as he sends them out (Matt. 10).

The theological concept of blessing was not fully absorbed into the cultic institution but maintained its own independent course. The cultic institution gained its strength and consistency that lasted thousands of years because in it the pre-Israelite, magic elements of blessing were blended with the theological elements into a new unity. But the overcoming of the magical nature of the fulfillment of blessing meant that what God did was never identical with the operation of blessing. That is to say, God remained completely free in relation to the execution of blessing and was in no way bound by the blessing that was imparted in worship. This freedom of God to bless or not to bless found expression in what continued to be said about his blessing, set free from its ritual impartation in worship.

In Deuteronomy it becomes clear that since blessing was tied to the obedience of the people it was endangered, for God could refuse blessing if his people were disobedient, and could send a curse instead of a blessing. At this point we saw the connection with the prophetic proclamation of judgment.

Another, more severe crisis in the traditional concept of blessing resulted from the destruction of the temple, the state, and the institutions of community life. Blessing came of necessity to be more and more tied to the obedience and piety of the individual, as in Deuteronomy it had been tied to the obedience of the people. Experience gradually made it clear that the theological belief about the dependence of blessing on obedience was no longer valid. There were more and more occasions on which it was not the pious who seemed to be blessed but the godless and wicked, while the pious had to suffer. This crisis of the concept of blessing is seen in a large number of psalms, and with special urgency in Psalm 73. The book of Job arose in this crisis and must be understood in terms of it. In the light of the history of blessing, Job signifies that the traditional theology of blessing, that is, the belief that God's blessing is connected with obedience, no longer corresponds to reality. The blessing that God imparts is not at our disposal; God can be on the side of those who are unblessed. By breaking out of traditional theological views of blessing in this way the book of Job points beyond the Old Testament.

BLESSING IN APOCALYPTIC LITERATURE

A full presentation of blessing in apocalyptic literature is beyond the scope of this work and would require an independent study. I shall merely indicate the role that blessing plays there. In the unfolding of the apocalyptic drama that begins with the final struggle between God and the powers of godlessness, there is generally a final parting of the ways; God's foes are eternally damned and God's people enter eternal glory. Wherever this eternal glory of God's people or of the pious is depicted, the apocalypses use the language of blessing. Nothing else is possible, because the ultimate, eternal glory is conceived of as totally static. All powers of destruction, disruption, and doom are overcome (Isa. 27:1), and thus in the culmination there can no longer be any salvation in the sense of rescue, deliverance, or liberation. To speak of "eternal salvation" is to speak of salvation only in the sense of blessing, and for this reason the language of blessing is used. This includes such features of the final state as a meal (Isa. 25:6), eternal peace (Isa. 26:12), the messianic kingdom of peace (Isa. 11; Zech. 9:9–10), prosperity and success (Jer. 27:6; Zech. 9:17; Isa. 66:11).

A typical presentation of this eternal salvation is found in Isaiah 65:20–23, where the language of blessing is pervasive.

> No more shall there be in it
>> an infant that lives but a few days,
>> or an old man who does not fill out his days,

for the child shall die a hundred years old,
   and the sinner a hundred years old shall be accursed.
They shall build houses and inhabit them;
   they shall plant vineyards and eat their fruit.
They shall not build and another inhabit;
   they shall not plant and another eat;
for like the days of a tree shall the days of my people be,
   and my chosen shall long enjoy the work of their hands.
They shall not labor in vain,
   or bear children for calamity;
for they shall be the offspring of the blessed of the Lord,
   and their children with them.

Here we encounter again the familiar vocabulary, "for they shall be the offspring of the blessed of the Lord" (23b). In a similar context in the New Testament this phrase is found in the pericope of the final judgment: "Then the King will say to those at his right hand, 'Come, O blessed of my father . . .' " (Matt. 25: 34a). It is the same designation in the same context. The occurrence of the word *blessed* in this context is not of itself decisive. What is decisive is that the portrayal of final salvation in the nature of the final culmination has the characteristics of a description of blessing. Eternal peace for all, including animals (Isa. 65:25), prosperity, eternal security, and tranquillity are the essential features. This corresponds to the fact that the final culmination has cosmic dimensions—the new heavens and the new earth, the end of the groaning of creation.

BLESSING IN THE NEW TESTAMENT

Two Insights Gained from the Old Testament

In the preliminary survey (pp. 24 ff., above) only the specific terminology was considered. The result of the survey indicated that it is not possible to say that blessing plays an essential or even substantial role in the New Testament. The only passage where blessing is prominent is the mission of the disciples in the Synoptics (Matt. 10 and parallels).

When we turn to the New Testament statements about blessing and see them in the light of the concept of blessing found in the Old Testament, the overview of the history of the concept helps us recognize the way in which the conception in the New

Testament fits into the context of tradition history. In addition to this, two specific insights have emerged that are essential for the evaluation of the New Testament concept but that cannot be derived from the New Testament alone.

(a) For the history of the Old Testament concept of blessing, the most significant development was the incorporation of blessing into the history of God's people accomplished by the Yahwist and in the Balaam pericopes. This is seen most clearly in the combining of blessing with promise. Here a prehistoric concept was borrowed and basically transformed by taking on a new dimension of historical extension in that it was now a blessing that God promises to bestow in the future (Gen. 12:1–3; see above, p. 51). In a similar way we can regard the New Testament usage of the concept of blessing as an incorporation of pre-Christian blessing into the Christ event, that is, as a Christianization of blessing. For the Yahwist the decisive change was that Yahweh became the one who blesses (a corresponding theologization of cursing did not take place in the Old Testament), all the activity of blessing became Yahweh's activity, and all the power of blessing, Yahweh's power (this is particularly clear in Num. 22–24). In much the same way in the New Testament the decisive change was that the blessing of Yahweh, the God of Israel, became blessing in Christ. Christ himself became the one who blesses, and all of God's bestowal of blessing became connected with God's work in Christ. In the Priestly Document the blessing given at the sanctuary, as it had been in pre-Israelite times and outside Israel, was transformed by the encounter at Sinai into the blessing of Yahweh, the blessing that Yahweh bestows on his people at the conclusion of worship (Num. 6:22–27). In much the same way in Christian worship the activity of bestowing blessing was adopted as the conclusion of worship, and in addition it was Christianized by the use of the sign of the cross. The significant question is the theological meaning of this process and what light this casts on the manner in which the New Testament statements about blessing are to be understood.

When we examine the relevant New Testament passages from this vantage point, a grouping of passages becomes at once apparent. One group of passages speaks of blessing in such a way that the echoes of the Old Testament statements about blessing are unmistakable. In them the heritage is stronger than its transformation (e.g., Mark 10:13–16; Luke 24:50). In the other group the transformation, the "Christianization" of blessing, is dominant (e.g., Rom. 15:29; Eph. 1:3).

It is not a matter of playing one group of passages off against the other, or of regarding one as negative and the other as positive. Rather it is important to recognize that the two groups exist side by side and to look for the significance of this fact. Here a comparison with the reformulation of the concept of blessing in the Yahwist source is of help. As we have seen, when the Yahwist incorporated blessing into history by means of the concept of the promise of blessing, he did not expunge the traditional concept but let it continue alongside the new formulation, so that we find in the patriarchal narratives two conceptions of blessing that really cannot be reconciled with each other. The Yahwist had the wisdom to see that a simple usurpation of the place of the old concept of blessing would not do justice to the new concept, and so in the new theological formulation he allowed the old concept of blessing to continue to speak.

We can approach the existence of the two differing groups of passages in the New Testament in the same way. There is a decidedly new formulation in which the word *blessing* characterizes God's saving activity in Christ. This formulation, however, allows for the possibility that the traditional concept of blessing could continue and have its own place even in the writings of the New Testament.

If this is recognized, then the exegete can no longer be satisfied simply to establish a categorical division between what is pre-Christian and what is genuinely Christian. He will no longer be content to subordinate one group to the other, but in dealing with each passage he will inquire into the place it should occupy in the course of development from the old concept to the new. It will then be apparent that there are many points of transition, that a passage cannot always be assigned to one group or the other, and that in any case it is not simply a matter of the Christianization of the concept of blessing in the sense of a usurpation by something new, but that the heritage of the traditional concept was respected.

(b) In the investigation of blessing in the Old Testament, we found that we could not restrict our efforts to the occurrence of the term *bless, blessing* or to the history of the term. We saw that God's activity of blessing and the results that came from it could not be confined to this term but involved a semantic domain that included a number of other terms, such as "multiply," "mature," "succeed," "bear fruit," and even "peace" and "presence." We saw also that God's blessing was connected with his work as Creator (Gen. 1:28 and the realization of blessing in the genealogies), and that wisdom was brought into relation with blessing. Similarly, the investigation of blessing in the New Testament cannot be confined to passages where the terms *eulogein* and *eulogia* occur but must move beyond them to look at the entire phenomenon of blessing as it is expressed in the wider semantic domain, as it is expressed in relationship to creation, and as it is seen in connection with wisdom.

In the Old Testament, blessing includes not only the act of bestowing blessing but also the way it operated in all its possibilities. As a result of the historicizing of blessing by the Yahwist, God's work of blessing came to share in the total relationship of God to his people. It operates in the vertical dimension of successive generations (in the family and in the nation) and in the horizontal dimension of the well-being of a community, which is what the Old Testament means by "peace." Whenever we inquire into the meaning of blessing in the Old Testament, we must not neglect this part of the total relationship of God to his people that is represented by blessing and its significance.

This provides us with another point of view that can help us understand what the New Testament means by blessing. We must ask whether the message of the New Testament is exclusively restricted to God's saving activity in Christ, or whether it does not have some relationship to the realm of blessing, that is, to growth, maturity, prosperity, and the bearing of fruit, in other words, to well-being.

We must ask what is the relationship between blessing and the acts of Jesus that bring a healing, protecting, prospering of the "natural man," and what relationship they bear to salvation.

We must ask how the work of the Creator is connected with blessing in the New Testament, and whether and in what way the New Testament statements about Creator and creation are related to the bestowal of blessing by God or by Christ.

We must ask what the New Testament means when it speaks of a constant activity within the boundaries of God's work of salvation, for instance, in those parables of Jesus in which growth and maturing are so significant, and then, too, in the Epistles, where the writers speak of continuing, of growing, of bearing fruit in the community. A study of the Beatitudes should be included also.[49]

By keeping in mind the meaning that these two points of view have for our understanding of the New Testament statements about blessing, we will be able to make use of the results of our study of the concept in the Old Testament.

WOLFGANG SCHENK, *Der Segen im Neuen Testament*: A DISCUSSION AND EVALUATION

Before examining these two points of view, it will be helpful to discuss and evaluate briefly the most recent study of blessing in the New Testament, Wolfgang Schenk's *Der Segen im Neuen Testament*.[50] It is based on his dissertation at the University of Jena.

Schenk begins with a discussion and evaluation of previous studies of blessing (pp. 1–32). He looks at the earliest studies of the Old Testament material by Mowinckel and Hempel; the earliest studies of the New Testament material, chiefly L. Brun's

---

49. Cf. J. Y. Campbell, "Blessedness," *IDB* 1: 445–46; Walter J. Harrelson, "Blessing and Cursings," ibid., p. 447: "In the NT the term *makarios* is the equivalent of the Hebrew *ashre* (Matt. 5:3–11, etc.; cf. Ps. 1:1 and the Septuagint usage), while the verb *eulegeo* probably stands for the Hebrew and Aramaic verb *brk*." See also W. Janzen, "*Ashre* in the Old Testament," *HTR* 58/2 (1965): 215–26, where he investigates the relationship between *ashre* and *brk* and its derivatives.

50. Berlin, 1967.

Segen und Fluch im Urchristentum,[51] Hermann W. Beyer's article in Kittel's *TWNT* and "Sketches for the Biblical Basis for a Theological Understanding of Blessing," in H. Echternach's *Segnende Kirche,*[52] Friedrich Horst's "Segen und Segenshandlungen in der Bibel,"[53] Ethelbert Stauffer's "Die sakramentale Bedeutung des kirchlichen Segens,"[54] E. Klessmann's "Was heisst segnen nach der Heiligen Schrift?"[55] Claus Westermann's "Die Frage nach dem Segen"[56] and the article "Segen und Fluch" in EKL,[57] and H. Köster's "Segen und Fluch im NT."[58]

Schenk then discusses the use of the words *eulogein* and *eulogia* in the New Testament. In section A he presents the statistics on the usage in the New Testament (pp. 33–35). The words and their derivatives are found 68 times (44 times as a verb, 16 as a substantive, and 8 as an adjective). Variations in usage are identified as follows:

Subject	Object
I. God	Man
II. Man	Man
III. Man	God

The most frequent usage (40 passages) is in the doxologies (III). Blessing as the action of God (I) is found in 19 passages, and as an activity between humans (II) in 6 passages.

In section B Schenk reports that the roots of the New Testament usage are basically to be found in the previous usage of the Greek term, but the original Greek meaning, "to use beautiful language," is found in the New Testament only in Romans 16:18. In all other instances the New Testament concept goes back to the Septuagint usage of *eulogein*, which was intended to render the Hebrew *brk*. The transition was probably the use in doxolo-

51. Oslo, 1932.
52. 1941; 2d ed. 1948.
53. *EvTh* 7 (1947–48) : 23–37, reprinted in *ThB* 12 (1961) : 188–202.
54. *Viva vox Evangelii: Festschrift für Bischof Meiser* (1951) , pp. 224ff.
55. *MPTh* 48 (1959) : 26–39.
56. *ZdZ* 11 (1957) : 244ff.
57. Vol. 3, pp. 916ff.
58. *RGG*³ 5: 1651–52.

gies, which the other occurrences then followed. "The concept and the activity had their origin in the culture of the Ancient Near East" (p. 38). "In the New Testament, with the exception of Romans 16:18, the concept is always derived from Old Testament usage" (p. 40). Thus, for example, Hebrews 11:20–21 is seen in terms of an Old Testament bestowal of blessing, but "a specifically New Testament understanding of blessing cannot be extracted from Hebrews 11:20–21."

In section C Schenk investigates the New Testament concept (pp. 42–130). Under heading I, the concept as a designation of the activity of God, he distinguishes between Christological passages dealing with the present and those dealing with the future. The first category includes Galatians 3:8–9, 14; Acts 3:25–26; Romans 15:29; Ephesians 1:3; Hebrews 7:1–7; Luke 24:50–51; the second includes Matthew 25:34; Hebrews 6:7–8; 1 Peter 3:9; Hebrews 12:17; 6:14.

In all these passages, blessing signifies God's saving activity in Christ. "God's blessing is understood as justification" (p. 43, in commenting on Gal. 3:8–9). "Christ is the fulfillment in salvation history of the promise to Abraham" (p. 47, in reference to Acts 3:25–26). In Romans 15:29, the "expression *eulogia Christou* is the culmination of the Christological usage of the concept of salvation in the New Testament" (p. 48). In Ephesians 1:3 the divine bestowal of blessing includes "election, redemption, grace, and revelation" (p. 51). On Matthew 25:34 he says: "Here God's blessing is precisely his eschatological, future act of justification" (p. 59). "To 'inherit blessing' means the future culmination of salvation" (p. 63, on 1 Pet. 3:9). In Hebrews 6:14 blessing is "the paradigm of future, final salvation in Christ" (p. 65). Blessing is "final salvation based on the resurrection of Jesus" (p. 63).

The conclusions of Schenk's study are clear. In all the passages in this group "blessing" is synonymous with salvation. For example, on page 64 he writes, "salvation (blessing)"; the nuances are to be found in the context, which may speak of the salvation in Christ in various ways. The equating of blessing and salvation is in all instances the same.

Under heading II he deals with the concept as a designation of an activity between one human and another. Three groups of passages are examined: Jesus blesses the children (Mark 10:16 and parallels); we are exhorted to "bless those who curse you" (Luke 6:28; 1 Cor. 4:12; Rom. 12:14; 1 Pet. 3:9); and Jesus speaks to the disciples as he sends them out (Matt. 10:12–13; Luke 10:5–6). In this section pronouncements of judgment outweigh exegetical conclusions. The statement "So we reach the same negative judgment" (p. 71) is typical of the entire section.

Joachim Jeremias explained the blessing of the children in terms of the custom of asking a rabbi on the Day of Atonement to place his hand on the head of one's children and to pray for them, and Schenk adopts this view (pp. 66–67). This results in the negative conclusion, "Blessing is peripheral and unemphasized" (p. 71). To sum up, the blessing of the children in Mark 10:16 "is to be understood entirely as intercession" (p. 72). "The early church did not practice any such pronouncements of blessing" (p. 73).

The second group (Luke 6:28, etc.) "speaks unambiguously of petition" (p. 76). The heading for the discussion of Jesus' commission to the disciples (Matt. 10; Luke 10) ends with a question mark. The procedure has nothing to do with blessing. "*Eirēnē* (in the greeting, 'Peace be on this house') expresses the concept of the salvation which God bestows" (p. 95). In addition, the section heading "New Testament Epistolary Greetings?" is automatically supplied with a question mark. "The greetings at the beginning and end of the New Testament letters are by no means specifically early Christian liturgical formulas for blessing, but are only petitions with a Christian content" (p. 92).

I shall not deal at any length here with the third part of Schenk's work, "The Concept as Designation for Doxology" (pp. 96–130).

Schenk presents the following conclusions:

(a) As God's action in relation to men, blessing in the New Testament is consistently a secondary concept for eschatological salvation or the eschatological gift of salvation in Christ" (p. 131). "A comprehensive view of these eleven passages makes it clear that in contrast to the Old Testament, blessing is always used in a soteriological sense. . . . It is not possible to construct a unified and comprehensive concept of blessing in the New Testament from these passages. . . . They show that the concept is found in the New Testament only as traditional Old Testament, Jewish material and no longer has any meaning of its own" (p. 132).

(b) As an action between humans, (1) "The blessing of the children can be identified merely as petition. . . . That there was no interest in blessing is demonstrated by the fact that specific bestowals of blessing were simply not present in the early church" (p. 132).

(2) The command "Bless those who curse you" means pray for them. "No other type of activity was possible. When the cause of love for one's enemies took over the concept of blessing, this constituted the end of blessing in the Old Testament sense" (p. 132).

(3) "This new role of blessing as petition . . . excludes any possible cultic role for blessing. . . . In Christianity the concept of blessing is to be subordinated to petition" (p. 133).

It was with great expectation that I began to read this first comprehensive and detailed investigation of the concept of blessing in the New Testament. I put it down with disappointment and sadness. This investigation of a New Testament concept that is found in a large number of passages in many areas of the New Testament and in quite different contexts produces in the end a totally negative result. It concludes "that the concept is found in the New Testament merely as traditional material of a concept in Old Testament and Jewish thought, but no longer has any distinctive meaning" (p. 132). It is dead, merely the "material of a concept."

What is particularly disappointing is that the investigation nowhere attempts to move beyond the negative conclusion that we are dealing only with the material of a concept that has no distinctive meaning. The writer never asked the question which necessarily arises from that conclusion, "Why then was the word used at all in the New Testament?" He is completely content with the conclusion that the concept has no meaning in the New Testament. He seems unaware of the consequence that the New Testament writers who used the concept lose considerable credibility thereby. They say "blessing" but do not mean "blessing." According to the writer, when they say blessing they mean justification, spirit, "the spiritual action of the exalted Lord in the execution of his proclamation" (p. 49). In Ephesians 1:3 the word means election, redemption, grace, revelation (p. 51). To be "heirs of blessing" is the future consummation of salvation or the paradigm of future salvation through Christ (p. 65). As the designation of an action between humans, blessing means petition (pp. 69ff.).

This amazing conclusion is the result of the one-sidedness of his exegesis. Schenk does not ask how it was that the New Testament writers came to use the concept of blessing in the various contexts in which it occurs. He does not ask where the concept came from, what road it traveled, or how it changed on that road. Nor does he ask what relation the various usages of the term have to each other, or whether within the New Testament we can detect differences in the usage of the term so that different stages or phases of usage could be recognized, as, for example, that the usage in the Synoptics was superseded by that in the Epistles. In his introduction Schenk states: "In none of the works that I have examined is the opinion represented that any of the New Testament writers had a distinctive concept of blessing. As a result, the presentation of my study cannot be organized according to the occurrence of the concept in the separate New Testament writings. . . . That question cannot be made a principle of the investigation" (p. 32).

In this way the writer has a priori excluded the possibility of finding traces of a history of the concept or even of finding various possibilities of understanding it or groups of similar interpretations in the various writings of the New Testament. Rather, *before* he begins his research he is convinced that all examples of its usage in the New Testament stand on the same level. This prejudgment is seen in the fact that in organizing the three large groups of passages he draws indiscriminately and at will from all the New Testament writings. It seems to me that this method of research is methodologically unjustifiable.

The failure to work from the point of view of tradition history is particularly clear at one point. If the concept in the New Testament no longer had any distinctive meaning but was still used rather frequently, Schenk believed this was because it was a "traditional term" (p. 35). He says this explicitly: "In the New Testament the concept is always determined by its usage in the Old Testament" (p. 40).

But how can anyone understand the usage of the concept in the New Testament while ignoring the content and usage it brought with it from the Old Testament? The writer is aware of this prehistory of the concept, but he never brought it to bear on his exegesis. The meaning of blessing in the New Testament can be discovered and explained only if the term is exegeted in the New Testament in terms of tradition history, and here that means in terms of the shaping of the concept by its prehistory in the Old Testament. The conclusion of Schenk's study, that blessing has no distinctive meaning in the New Testament but is there only as "traditional material of a concept," is predetermined by his ignoring the prehistory in which the concept is shaped. Because of this basic methodological failure, the conclusions of his work cannot be accepted.

His work does have its positive points, however. Schenk shows that the New Testament does not explicitly speak of or systematically develop as a theme either the bestowal of blessing by God or Christ or the giving of a blessing in worship. It shows further that the writings of the New Testament are not sufficiently interested in blessing in its specific and original meaning to give it a particular emphasis. Schenk also rightly stressed that in a variety of passages the word is found in an altered sense and does not represent Christ's activity of blessing but rather his saving action. But it cannot be demonstrated that this is the case in all passages where the word is found in the New Testament. The usefulness of this study seems to me to be that it shows how difficult it is to find in any of the New Testament passages that speak of blessing a basis for bestowing blessing as a function of the church, and how unavoidable is the question of finding a biblical basis for this function.

In several places the writer goes beyond his exegetical conclusions and comments that "it is clear that we must deny the possibility that there was any particular bestowal of blessing in the community of Jesus Christ in the first century" (p. 133). He makes that assertion not once but repeatedly and with emphasis. In another place he writes in reference to Luke 6:28:

> Jesus uses the word to mean "petition." . . . The early church accepted this formulation of Jesus and preserved it. Except for this, no other bestowal of blessing was possible, because there was no other possible understanding of blessing. The appropriation of the concept of blessing for love for one's enemies meant the end of blessing in the priestly sense it had in the Old Testament" (p. 132) .

The writer asserts that the Christian church of the first century knew no other type of blessing, even that the usage of the term in the New Testament excluded the possibility of any other. Note the remarkable situation. The concept here has on the one hand no distinctive meaning, is merely traditional material for a concept; but on the other hand it is said to have such far-reaching influence that it goes beyond the realm of exegesis.

Schenk's study concludes that blessing in worship and in other activities of the church is unscriptural. But it is not possible to draw this conclusion from the exegesis that he presents, nor is his exegetical basis as such reliable. Any examination of Schenk's work must proceed from the results of the study of the Old Testament.

The division of passages that Schenk makes must be corrected. Leaving aside the passages in which *eulogein* means "praise," there are three groups: God as the one who blesses (I); Christ as the one who blesses (II); humans as those who bless (III). The second group is missing in Schenk's work, because he assigns one of the passages that belong here to I and one to III. This new division also changes the totals at which Schenk arrived.

God as the One Who Bestows Blessing (Schenk's I)

This usage of the term is found in nine passages in the New Testament, and in several the term is used more than once (fifteen times in all). One passage in the Gospels (Matt. 25:34), one in Acts (3:25–26), two in the letters of Paul (Rom. 15:29; Gal. 3:8–9, 14), three in Hebrews (6:7–8; 6:14; 12:17), and once each in Ephesians 1:3 and 1 Peter 3:9.

(a) One group quotes and comments on Genesis 12:1–3 or Genesis 22:17–18: Galatians 3:8–9, 14; Acts 3:25–26; and Hebrews 6:14.

Galatians:

> And the scripture, foreseeing that God would justify the Gentiles by faith, preached the gospel beforehand to Abraham, saying, "In you shall all the nations be blessed." So then, those who are men of faith are blessed with Abraham who had faith . (3:8–9)

> Christ redeemed us from the curse of the law, . . . that in Christ Jesus the blessing of Abraham might come upon the Gentiles, that we might receive the promise of the Spirit through faith. (3:13–14)

Acts:

> You are the sons of the prophets and of the covenant which God gave to your fathers, saying to Abraham, "And in your posterity shall all the families of the earth be blessed." God, having raised up his servant, sent him to you first, to bless you in turning every one of you from your wickedness. (3:25–26)

Hebrews:

> For when God made a promise to Abraham, since he had no one greater by whom to swear, he swore by himself, saying, "Surely I will bless you and multiply you." And thus Abraham, having patiently endured, obtained the promise. (6:13–15)

In examining this group of passages, we should note first of all that they speak of God's bestowal of blessing in connection with the promise of blessing to Abraham, that is, in connection with the passage where the transformation of the concept of blessing by the Yahwist is expressed through the connection of blessing with promise. This underlines what was said in relation to the first conclusion from the study of blessing in the Old Testament—in the history of the concept of blessing the two most important transformations are the one made by the Yahwist and the one in the New Testament. In the quotations in this group of passages, the connection of the concept of blessing with the work of Christ is related to the connection of blessing with the promise in Genesis 12 (or Gen. 22).

Both Galatians 3 and Acts 3 expressly declare that the promise to Abraham is fulfilled in Christ. Hebrews 6:14, however, presupposes that the promise to Abraham had already been fulfilled; in his patient waiting for the promise, Abraham is a model for the early church. Thus only the first two passages can be considered as evidence of the Christianization of the concept of blessing.

Galatians 3 is the most important passage for this Christianization of the concept. Here Paul explicitly states that for him Genesis 12:3 proclaims in advance the justification of the Gentiles through faith. He understands the promise "In you shall all the nations be blessed" as being equivalent to "shall be justified." And when Paul in verse 9 draws the conclusion, "So then those who are men of faith are blessed with Abraham who had faith," "blessed" here is for him a synonym for "justified." In the same way in verses 13–14, "the promise of the Spirit through faith" is synonymous with the "blessing of Abraham," which in Jesus Christ has come to the Gentiles. For Paul, then, what was promised to Abraham and fulfilled in Christ is no longer blessing, but justification in Christ through faith. Heinrich Schlier says that here "Blessing is the activity of the God who justifies."[59] This means that here we have a conscious and emphatic transformation of the Old Testament concept of blessing. In the fulfillment of the promise, the blessing of God was transformed into God's saving deeds in Christ. I agree with Schenk when in his discussion of this passage he concludes: "In Galatians 3 Paul's understanding of the way the promise to Abraham was fulfilled in Christ shows no appreciable difference between the act of being blessed and justification (vv. 8–9) and between the gift of blessing and the Spirit (v. 14)" (p. 46). I cannot, however, agree with his further conclusion that as a consequence of this the word *blessing* has in this passage lost for Paul any distinctive meaning. It could hardly be the case that Paul dealt with Genesis 12:1–3 in such great detail in order to express the idea that the blessing promised to Abraham is no blessing at all. The point of the discussion of the promise to Abraham can only be that Paul sees in some sense a positive connection between the promise made to Abraham and its fulfillment in Christ. It means that what was promised to Abraham was to extend to the Gentiles. Thus there is for Paul

---

59. *Der Brief an die Galater* (1951), p. 89.

a positive connection between the promise of blessing to Abraham and the fulfillment of that promise in the message of salvation in Christ, which is to include the Gentiles. When the blessing promised to Abraham is transformed into God's saving action in Christ, the context is that of the activity of God which connects the promise with its fulfillment.

The same holds true for Peter's speech in Acts 3:25–26. The promise to Abraham (in the repetition of Gen. 12:1–3 in Gen. 22:17–18) is explained as having been fulfilled in Christ, and in similar manner "blessing" is a synonym for God's saving activity in Christ. Here too the Old Testament concept of salvation is basically transformed, and here too the purpose of the reference to the promise to Abraham is to show a connection between it and the fulfillment that has now taken place. "Christ [is] the fulfillment in salvation history of the promise to Abraham" (Schenk, p. 47). The correspondence in Galatians 3 and Acts 3 of these two features, (1) transformation of God's blessing into the saving deeds of God in Christ and (2) emphasis on the connection between both as acts in salvation history, leads us to assume in relation to both passages that there existed in early Christianity a tradition that understood Genesis 12:1–3 in this way.

(b) In a second group of passages we will endeavor to see if there is the same or similar use of "blessing" without the citation of Genesis 12.

Ephesians 1:3:

> Blessed be the God and Father of our Lord Jesus Christ, who has blessed us in Christ with every spiritual blessing in the heavenly places.

The use of the word *blessing* in Ephesians 1:3 is very close to Galatians 3, in spite of other differences in language. Here too "blessing" is consciously and emphatically used to designate God's work of deliverance in Christ, and this is then developed in verses 4–14. This means that there is here a definite Christianization of the concept of blessing. The "spiritual blessing in Christ," for which the introduction to the Epistle praises God, is the work of redemption that God has accomplished for us in Christ. Here too this blessing is understood as an inheritance: "the guarantee of our inheritance" (v. 14), and this looks back to a preceding activity of God (vv. 9–10, "the fulness of time"). Blessing is thus understood entirely in Christological or even soteriological terms. "Spiritual blessing" means "this blessing is the Spirit" (Schenk, p. 50).[60] God's work of redemption in Christ is termed "blessing" in order to indicate its connection with the blessing that had been promised (v. 11), and the text does not intend to say more than this.

(c) Several passages speak of "inheriting" the blessing.

1 Peter 3:9: ". . . But on the contrary bless, for to this you have been called, that you may obtain [Gr. "inherit"] a blessing."

Hebrews 12:17: "For you know that afterward, when he [Esau] desired to inherit the blessing, he was rejected . . ."

Hebrews 6:7–8: "For land which has drunk the rain . . . receives a blessing from God."

Hebrews 6:12: "So that you may not be sluggish, but imitators of those who through faith and patience inherit the promises."

Hebrews 6:15: "And thus Abraham, having patiently endured, obtained the promise."

These passages lead us to the conclusion that in early Christian paranesis (each of these passages is part of a paranesis) "to inherit blessing" was a bound phrase. This can be seen most clearly in 1 Peter 3:9, "for to this you have been called, that you may obtain a blessing." It is presupposed in Hebrews 12:17 and can be seen also in Hebrews 6. Inheritance of the blessing means the attaining of eschatological salvation. Schenk says (p. 63): " 'Inherit blessing' . . . is an expression that designates the future culmination of salvation; both its elements are drawn from the tradition of the Old Testament and early Judaism." The Epistle to the Hebrews refers "inherit blessing" to events in the Old Testament. Hebrews

60. There in n. 191 Schenk refers to a work of mine and his discussion of that work on pp. 29–30. The reference makes it clear enough that I said there that only if Eph. 1:3 were the only New Testament explanation of blessing could be there anything questionable about using the blessing in Num. 6 in Christian worship. But I cannot agree with Schenk when he continues: "This means that beside the Spirit there is no longer any other blessing in the original sense of a distinctive gift of God. Any other content for the concept of blessing is ruled out" (p. 50) . I do not find in Eph. 1:3–14 any polemical tendency against an existing concept of blessing.

12:17 says that Esau wanted to inherit the blessing, and in chapter 6 the readers are challenged to imitate the example of Abraham, to whom blessing and riches were promised and who by patient waiting attained what had been promised. This is expressed in the exhortation "Imitate the example of those who through faith and patient waiting inherited those things that had been promised." "Inherit blessing," "inherit promises," and "attain to what has been promised" are thus in this context synonymous.

In these passages also the concept of blessing has been Christianized, but not in the same sense as those in the first group. Since they deal with a "designation of the future culmination of salvation," blessing is not, as in the first group, the redeeming work of Christ or the saving action of God but is the salvation made possible through this deed of deliverance, seen as a future culmination of salvation and well-being.

It cannot therefore be said of this group as of the first group that the Old Testament concept of salvation has been thoroughly transformed. On the contrary, these passages are very close to the Old Testament concept.

This is seen in 1 Peter 3:9, when the following verse introduces with the conjunction "for" a quotation of Psalm 34:13–17 that begins, "He that would love life and see good days." In Hebrews 12:17 it is said that Esau wanted to inherit the blessing, and so here "inherit blessing" can designate something that happened in the days of the fathers, as is also true in Hebrews 6:12, 14, where even Abraham inherited the promised blessing. The blessing at work in creation, that is, blessing as the power of fertility, can serve as a symbol of this: "For land which has drunk the rain . . . and brings forth vegetation . . . receives a blessing from God" (Heb. 6:7). This illustration shows that the author of Hebrews continued to hold to the original understanding of blessing.

The description of salvation in the language of blessing as found in the later oracles of the Old Testament, in apocalyptic, and in early Jewish literature constitutes the basis of all passages that speak of "inheriting blessing." This connects them with the usage in Matthew 25:34, which is based on Isaiah 65:23b and is either a quotation of or an allusion to that passage. In the description of the consummation of salvation in Isaiah 65:16b–25, the people of God of the final days are called "the offspring of the blessed of the Lord" (Isa. 65:23). This is an Old Testament expression from the late period of prophecies of salvation and is close to apocalyptic language. In it the time of the culmination is portrayed in the language of blessing. No specifically Christological or soteriological meaning can be found in this group of passages.

On the basis of these passages the question must be broadened to read "What language does the New Testament use when it speaks of the culmination of salvation as a condition?" On the basis of the Old Testament statements, it is clear that in every portrayal of a future state of salvation the vocabulary of blessing predominates. This is true also of apocalyptic. The specific form there is the portrayal of salvation, which, as distinct from a declaration of salvation (perfect tense) and a proclamation of salvation (imperfect), depicts the condition of accomplished salvation as an unlimited state of being blessed (see above). What is the relation of this to the New Testament? I cannot answer that question here, but pose it for New Testament scholars.

(d) Romans 15:29 reads, "I know that when I come to you I shall come in the fulness of the blessing of Christ." Schenk has this to say of this passage: "The use here of the expression 'blessing of Christ' marks the high point of the Christological use of the concept of blessing in the New Testament" (p. 48). He explains his statement in this way: "Thus we may conclude that Romans 15:29 means by the rich blessing of Christ the activity through the Spirit of the exalted Lord as his messengers carry out the work of proclamation" (p. 49). It is characteristic that in Schenk's explanation of this passage every specific meaning of the word *blessing* has been radically eliminated. Even here he does not pose the question, if Paul had meant that, why didn't he say it? "The high point of the Christological usage" is reduced to the point at which the phrase "blessing of Christ" means nothing at all. Paul is not attempting to formulate some teaching, as Schenk's explanation would indicate, but he is saying a personal word; he is speaking of his projected visit to Rome. The word *blessing* is a feature of such a visit of an apostle to a congregation, as Matthew 10 shows. For example, Ernst Käsemann says in connection with 1 Corinthians 16:22 that "the apostle as a representative of his heavenly lord possesses the power of blessing and curse."[61] When Paul says that he intends to go to the Romans in the fullness of the blessing of Christ, he is expressing the expectation that "the activity through the Spirit of the exalted Lord as his messengers carry out the work of proclamation" will accomplish something, that out of this proclamation something will grow and ripen, that his coming will serve the growth, maturing, and strengthening of the church.

The meaning of Romans 15:29 for the concept of blessing consists in the fact that the new expression "blessing of Christ" points to a new usage of the concept of blessing in the Christian church. The church speaks of blessing not only in order to express the expectation that the proclamation of the gospel will take place but also to express what the results will be, that is, to speak of the growth, prosperity, advancement, and strengthening of the church. This is the Old Testament concept of blessing in reference to a community, in the first instance, the people of God, and now the church of Jesus Christ, whose existence includes not only a series of events (proclamation and justification) but also of necessity a continuous occurrence; it means growth and faithfulness, becoming strong and maturing, progressing and abiding.

Here I shall pose another question for specialists in the New Testament. What is the relationship in the New Testament between what it says on the one hand about God's activity that is of a punctiliar nature, such as the proclaiming and the hearing of the Word (proclamation), justification, forgiveness of sins, the Christ event as an eschatological occurrence, and so on, and what it says on the other hand about events that have an entirely different structure, persevering, progressing and declining, growing and maturing, activities, that is, that according to their nature are not specific events?

I pose this question in reference to those passages in the New

---

61. *Exegetische Versuche und Besinnungen* 2: 72.

Testament where God is the one who blesses. Three groups of passages represent this usage. (1) Galatians 3:8–9, 14; Acts 3:25–26; and Ephesians 1:3. In these passages the Old Testament concept of blessing is basically altered. "Blessing" means explicitly and emphatically God's saving act in Christ, or the justification wrought in this act. The concept thus has a Christological or soteriological meaning. The reason God's saving activity is called "blessing" in these three passages is that they portray the fulfillment of the promises of blessing given to the patriarchs. In Galatians 3 and Acts 3 this point is made by reference to Genesis 12:1–3 (or 22:17–18), and Ephesians 1:3ff. only alludes to the Christ event as fulfillment. In this passage, however, the term *blessing* is partially characterized by the form of the Ephesian letter, which begins with a doxology (*eulogetos-eulogia*).

(2) A second group speaks of "inheriting blessing" (1 Pet. 3:9; Heb. 12:17; 6:7–8, 12–14). Here too the concept of blessing has been Christianized, but these passages are closer to the Old Testament usage. They are based on the description of the consummation of salvation in the language of blessing in the late Old Testament prophecies of salvation. Matthew 25:34, which is based on Isaiah 65:23b, is very close to this group.

(3) Romans 15:29 stands by itself. The new combination, "blessing of Christ," points to a new application of the concept of blessing in the Christian community, where the community is concerned with its growth, strength, and prosperity.

JESUS CHRIST IS THE ONE WHO BLESSES (SCHENK'S II)

These passages are Mark 10:16 and parallels; Luke 9:16; 24:30, 50–51; Hebrews 7:1–7. Only in the Synoptics do we find passages which report that Jesus bestowed blessing. But the blessing of Jesus is not entirely absent from the Epistles. In Romans 15:29, *eulogia Christou,* Christ is the subject of the verbal idea, but the passage actually speaks of the effect of the blessing bestowed by the Risen One. In Hebrews 7:1–7 Melchizedek is, as the one who blesses, a type of Christ.

(a) The blessing of the children occurs in Mark 10:13–16, Matthew 19:13–15, and Luke 18:15–17. Joachim Jeremias called attention to *Tractate Sopherim* 18:5, which mentions the custom of asking on the Day of Atonement for a rabbi to lay his hands on children and pray for them (Schenk, p. 67). Schenk exerts special effort to prove the meaninglessness of blessing in this text. His exegesis here is extremely tendentious and arouses the suspicion that the writer was after all impressed by the obviously unquestioning way in which the passage reports that Jesus blessed the children who were brought to him. L. Brun comments on the text:

> [It is here presupposed] that Jesus' words of blessing and his laying his hands on the children's heads had a direct effect that lasted beyond the moment. . . . Here too Jesus is the evangelist and the bearer of the kingdom of God. His blessing and the laying on of hands impart to the children in some way the kingdom itself.[62]

And Peter Brunner writes of this passage: "It cannot be disputed that in the understanding of the text of the Gospel this bestowal of blessing by the laying on of hands represents the exhibition of authority."[63]

It would not do to place too much stress on the significance of this passage for our understanding of blessing in the context of Jesus' activity, since in the parallels in Matthew and Luke the word itself is not used. But the simple mention in Mark of the fact that Jesus blessed the children, or in Matthew that he laid his hands on them, shows that in any case the evangelists in their portrayal of the work of Jesus regarded this blessing of the children as a possibility that required neither explanation nor justification. The important thing here for the concept of blessing is the fact that the children were blessed. The custom cited by Jeremias and the further parallels in Strack-Billerbeck show that it was "a normal activity of a Jewish father or a rabbi" (Schenk, p. 67). That is the important point. We have here, then, clearly and beyond dispute the concept of blessing that has come down from the Old Testament and from Jewish practice. Since it is children whom Jesus blesses here, the evangelists are bringing to our attention (and this is true of all three parallel accounts)

62. *Segen und Fluch im Urchristentum,* p. 20.
63. "Der Segen als dogmatisches und liturgisches Problem," in *Pro Ecclesia* (1966) , pp. 339–51, 345.

that the activity of Jesus was not limited to adults but was for the whole person. That means it was for men and women in their coming into being, their growth, and their maturing, as it was said of Jesus himself (Luke 2:52; cf. 1:80). That is precisely what blessing means—growth, and maturing, the health and well-being of children. Note that the scope of the saying is to be found not here but in the words which are directed to adults (Mark 10:15; Matt. 19:14b; Luke 18:17). With no particular emphasis and almost incidently, the pericope expresses the truth that in order to hear the proclamation of the kingdom of God and to respond to it a person must first be born, be a small child, and grow. The work of Jesus includes this creaturely side of our humanity, and therefore he is not only the one who saves and who proclaims salvation in the coming of the kingdom but is also the one who blesses.

When we move beyond this passage, where Jesus' bestowal of blessing is mentioned rather in passing, and investigate the meaning of blessing for the totality of the work of Jesus, we must not stop with the occurrences of the term but look at the whole phenomenon of blessing. We must ask where else and in what other ways in the Gospels we find this attention to the creaturely side of humanity. The question leads us to two types of material, first the miracles, especially those of healing, and then the sayings that speak of the protection and preservation of human life and that take seriously our nature as creatures, such as the saying in the Sermon on the Mount about being anxious.

We will then find present in both groups of passages the same structure that we saw in Mark 10:13–16. The emphasis of the saying or story lies on the *basileia*, the attaining to or entering into the kingdom. In the work of Jesus, however, this emphasis is related in a positive way to the bodily existence of persons, to their nature as creatures. It is there, for instance, in the account of a miracle of healing or of a word of forgiveness, and it is also there in the sayings about being anxious. This would require, however, an extensive investigation. For the meaning of the New Testament concept of blessing it should be emphasized that blessing, as it is presented in Mark 10 and in other passages, includes our human nature as creatures within the sphere of Jesus' work.

(b) The blessing spoken at a meal is found in the following passages:

Luke 9:16: "And taking the five loaves and the two fish he looked up to heaven, and blessed and broke them, and gave them to the disciples. . . ."

Luke 22:17: "And he took a cup, and when he had given thanks. . . ."

Luke 24:30: "When he was at table with them, he took the bread and blessed and broke it. . . ."

Here too we must be careful not to exaggerate the meaning of these passages (a complete list is given by Schenk in a table on p. 126). As in Mark 10:13–16, Jesus is not doing something that is in any way new. On the contrary, in blessing the bread he is continuing a traditional custom for which many instances could be cited (see Strack-Billerbeck on these passages). The many exegetes who stressed that in this blessing of the bread there is nothing specifically new, nothing specifically distinctive of the work of Jesus, were right. The important thing is that Jesus' observance of the custom seemed so important to Luke that he recorded it, even in the account of Jesus' last meal with his disciples. Here we find the same relationship between blessing and saving, or between blessing and the coming of the kingdom, that we found in different form in Mark 10:13–16. In the account of the Last Supper the Gospel writers saw in the bread and the wine not only that which they were to mean in the Christian eucharist but also that which they are in themselves—the fruits of the field which grew through the power of God's blessing and for which we are to give our humble thanks to the Creator. Luke gives particular emphasis to this aspect by using the wording of the ritual meal almost verbatim in the two other passages, where an ordinary meal is involved. Even the difference in vocabulary does not alter this fact.

The humble recognition of the Creator's blessing on the bread and the wine is brought to expression in the accounts of the Last Supper precisely there where the death of Jesus Christ for mankind is mentioned, that is, the savior's work of redemption.

(c) Luke 24:50–51: "Then he led them out as far as Bethany, and lifting up his hands he blessed them. While he blessed them, he parted from them." Schenk presents an exegetical discussion of this passage (pp. 54–56). He explains that the "special expressions of the passage (lifting up his hands, blessing, worship, and praise offered by the ones blessed) point, as Theodor Zahn had already seen, to the model of the Jewish priestly blessing" (p. 57). He refers to Leviticus 9:22–24, but finds a more precise model in Ecclesiasticus 50:19–22: "Luke structured the conclusion of his Gospel on the model of Sirach's book. P. A. van Stempvoort's demonstration of this should be conclusive. He wrote, 'We can find in Sirach 50 the literary background of Luke's description of the last Christophany.' "[64] Schenk concludes: "The Christ of the ascension is presented by Luke in stylized form as the high priest bestowing a blessing" (p. 58).

This exegesis is a typical example of a comparison of texts that rests content with a similarity of wording and either does not know the background of the passage in tradition history or does not try to discover it. The "literary background" is not sufficient if the exegete does not ask what are the contexts of both passages in terms of form history and tradition history. The above exegesis suppresses the fact that the situation in Luke 24:50–51 is basically different from that in Ecclesiasticus 50:19–22 and Leviticus 9:22–24. There the worship is concluded by the priest's blessing, and with this blessing the congregation, that is, those whom the priest has blessed, are sent away. In Luke 24:50–51, on the other hand, the disciples, who receive the blessing, are left behind and the one who bestowed the blessing is taken away. The statement that "the Christ of the ascension is presented by Luke in stylized form as the high priest bestowing a blessing" is not only false, but the idea of a high priest who is taken away after he bestows the blessing is absurd. It is not the priestly blessing that forms the background for Luke 24:50–51 but the blessing given in parting. It is entirely possible that the priestly blessing influenced the formulation of the wording (e.g., the lifting of hands), but that does not alter the fact that this is intended to be seen as a blessing at leave-taking. That is clear from the situation, and no particular

---

64. "The Interpretation of the Ascension in Luke and Acts," *NTSt* 5 (1958/59) : 30–42," in Schenk, *Der Segen im NT*, p. 34.

parallels are needed to establish it. Peter Brunner says of this passage:

> The risen and ascending Lord left his blessing behind with those who remained on earth. By this he bestows his peace, his salvation as a continuing presence in his church. The ascension necessarily raised the question of the presence of Christ. In Matthew the question is answered in the final words of Jesus, "Lo, I am with you always, to the close of the age" (Matt. 28:20b) . In Luke the answer is to be found in the promise of the Spirit and the blessing that follows immediately. There is a very close relationship between these two answers to the question of the presence of the Risen One. God's promise to Isaac in Genesis 26:3, "I will be with you, and will bless you," is a hendiadys; each statement is an interpretation of the other.[65]

I agree completely and have only a few comments to make.

The blessing which the Lord bestowed as he ascended has first of all the meaning that blessings at parting always have. The one who gives the blessing imparts a power that remains with those he leaves behind, and this power maintains the ties between those who are separated from each other.

The specific meaning in this special situation where the Lord parts from his community lies in the fact that it is this crucified and risen Lord who is leaving his blessing and his peace behind with his community, just as he said in the Gospel of John, without using the term *bless*, "Peace I leave with you; my peace I give to you" (John 14:27). If, as Peter Brunner has rightly observed, the statement in Matthew 28:20, which stands in the same position as John 14:27, "I am with you always," says essentially the same thing, it becomes clear that in Matthew, Luke, and John the same meaning is intended although the vocabulary is different.

The statements all refer to the same event, the moment of Jesus' departure from his disciples. In differing ways they all express the idea that the departure of Jesus is not the only thing that is to be stated here; rather, in spite of everything he remains with them "to the close of the age," and by bestowing his blessing he is leaving power with them.

Here, where the history of salvation is concluded, the work of

65. "Der Segen," p. 346.

salvation ended, where the savior has finished his saving act, a new relationship begins that can be described as his presence, his remaining with them, his blessing. This new relationship uses a new language, the language of blessing, which includes the terms *presence, remaining,* and *peace* just as much as it includes the term *blessing.*

Here I want to pose an additional question for New Testament scholars. It cannot be accidental that the three passages in Matthew, Luke, and John agree that at the point of transition from the drama of the history of salvation to the new relationship of the exalted Lord to his community, among whom the deliverance was accomplished, we find the language of the continuous activity of God, the language of blessing. It would be important to investigate the relation of the concepts used here—blessing, remaining, and presence—to the other concepts in the New Testament that depict the relationship of the risen Lord to his community, especially the Pauline term "in Christ." In the Gospel of John it is obvious that the language of the farewell discourse in chapters 13–17, which describes the relation of Jesus to his community after his departure, differs from that which described the events of Jesus' earthly life.

The question has far-reaching significance. If it is true that two types of language are used to say two different things, this would mean that the exalted Lord is present with his community not only in such events as the proclamation of the Word, the forgiveness of sins, and the call to discipleship, but also in his blessing which he left behind with the community; that is, in his being present with them to the close of the age in a continuous way not characterized by acts or events, that is, in the "blessing of Christ," of which Paul speaks in Romans 15:29.

If we bring together the passages in which Jesus is the one who blesses, the only group is composed of the passages that recount the blessing at a meal. One passage tells of the blessing of the children and one of the blessing of the disciples as he parts from them. This shows that there is no emphasis on the word, and it is used only seldom.

(1) The blessing of the children continues the tradition of the blessing bestowed by a father, and in later times by a rabbi. In the

biblical apothegm it is placed in a new context, but the act of blessing children is as such the same as in the Old Testament and in Jewish tradition. By blessing the children, Jesus includes the developing person in his work and so includes the creaturely side of humanity. The blessing of the children includes their growth and their prosperity.

(2) By blessing the bread, Jesus continued a traditional practice. In the Gospels this practice becomes a part of Jesus' last supper with his disciples and thus the fruits of the field that have grown through the power of God's blessing are received from the Creator in humble thankfulness. This is expressed precisely at the point where the Savior's work of redemption is introduced.

(3) Behind the blessing at Jesus' departure is the custom found in the Old Testament and in Jewish tradition of bestowing blessing at leave-taking. The specific meaning of blessing in this special situation is that the one who was crucified and has risen again, the Lord who has completed his work of deliverance for his community and for the world, remains united with his followers through the blessing that he leaves behind with them.

In every passage where Jesus bestows blessing, the concept is the same as in the Old Testament and in Jewish tradition. At the basis of them all is a procedure of blessing that Jesus simply took over when he blessed the children, blessed the bread, and blessed his disciples as he departed from them. The specific point of each event is that the one who blesses is the Lord, the Savior, the Christ. It is this that makes these events distinctive, not some transformation of the concept of blessing or of the way blessing is bestowed. This is related to the fact that in each passage the blessing is subordinated to an act that represents a saving event. In Mark 10 it is connected with the entering the Kingdom, in the blessing of the bread with the memorial meal, and in the parting blessing with the glorification of the Son of God. This illustrates clearly the difference between these passages and the group comprising Galatians 3, Acts 3, and Ephesians 1:3, where the blessing is identified with God's act of deliverance in Christ, in contrast to the subordination to the events of deliverance. But while subordinated, blessing is still not absorbed into salvation.

Schenk in his work eliminates the group of passages in which

Jesus is the one who blesses. He does this by subsuming Mark 10 under his group C II, "The Concept as Designation of Procedures Between Human Beings," Luke 24:50–51 under group C I, "The Concept as Designation of an Act of God," and the passages about blessing bread under C III, "The Concept as Designation of a Doxological Act" (pp. 125ff.).

PEOPLE BLESS OTHER PEOPLE (SCHENK'S III)

This group includes Hebrews 11:20–21, 7:1–7, Luke 6:28, 1 Corinthians 4:12, Romans 12:14, 1 Peter 3:9, Matthew 10:12–13, Luke 10:5–6, and the greetings in the Epistles. This is not a large list and the only grouping possible is of those that speak of blessing those who curse or persecute you. One person blessing another is thus an event found only rarely in the New Testament.

(a) In a few passages we have only the reminder that of old among God's people one person might bless another. Hebrews 11:20–21 reminds us that Isaac blessed Jacob and Esau and that Jacob blessed his sons. The author's purpose is to emphasize that this took place "in faith," in keeping with the way he portrays the entire history of God's people in ancient times as a history of faith. No connection is established between the patriarchal blessing and the author's own day.

In Hebrews 7:1–7 Abraham's being blessed by the high priest Melchizedek (Gen. 14) is interpreted typologically to illustrate the exalted position of Christ. The intent of the passage is merely to illustrate the typological relationship of Melchizedek to Christ, "the high priest after the order of Melchizedek." The text is not interested in the bestowal of blessing as such, and we can only say that as Hebrews 11:20–21 presupposes the blessing bestowed by the patriarch, this passage assumes the priestly blessing of the old covenant.

(b) The following passages concern blessing those who curse you:

"But I say to you that hear, Love your enemies, do good to those who hate you, bless those who curse you, pray for those who abuse you" (Luke 6:27–28).

"Bless those who persecute you; bless and do not curse them" (Rom. 12:14).

"When reviled, we bless; when persecuted, we endure; when slandered, we try to conciliate" (1 Cor. 4:12–13a).

"Do not return evil for evil or reviling for reviling; but on the contrary bless, for to this you have been called, that you may obtain a blessing" (1 Pet. 3:9).

In three of these four passages, "bless" is found in a paranesis, and in these three places it is a part of a contrasting set of terms.

"Bless those who curse you . . ." (Luke 6:28).

"Bless those who persecute you . . ." (Rom. 12:14).

"Do not return evil for evil . . . but on the contrary bless" (1 Pet. 3:9).

In the fourth passage it is also found in a set of contrasts, "When reviled, we bless" (1 Cor. 4:12), but here Paul is describing his life as an apostle (4:9–13). We may assume that Luke 6:28 gives the earliest form of the exhortation, and that in 1 Corinthians 4:12 the exhortation that Paul makes in Romans 12:14 stands in the background. In all the variations the contrast remains the same. Jesus' disciples are exhorted not to respond to curses, persecution, reviling, or abuse with the same type of language but with just the opposite. The words "Bless those who curse you" give the instruction in its most succinct form. We must thus interpret the word *bless* in terms of this contrast provided by love for our enemies. This contrast is presented in various ways—love, do good, bless, pray for—and this points to the varied possibilities of responding to hatred, contempt, curses, and insults. But this multiplicity of possibilities would be misinterpreted if we insisted on the precise content of each word. It means that if someone curses you, you should answer with the exact opposite. This indicates that the meaning of "bless" is quite wide here. It can mean doing good, showing a friendly attitude, speaking a gracious word, or it can also be intercession. In no case, however, is it possible to assign to the word *bless* the one, exclusive meaning of "intercession" in all four passages, as Schenk wants to do (pp. 76, 79). It would be possible to say that "Bless those who curse you" is an exhortation to love your enemies, but Schenk has no basis for asserting, as he does, that *"eulogein* in this context is the term for intercession" (p. 80).

For our understanding of the word *bless*, we can draw the conclusion that it is here determined by the contrast to curse, as in

the parallel exhortation "love your enemies," and "bless" signifies a friendly or helpful attitude toward the one who is cursing
or insulting you. There are many possibilities here that cannot
be determined more closely.

Here, too, there is something that resembles a Christianization
of blessing. It does not consist, as Schenk thinks, in the fact that
"*eulogein* was taken over from the cultic realm" (p. 80) and used
as a term for intercession. Schenk ignores the fact that in the Old
Testament "blessing" was a living reality outside the cultic realm
as well as within it. It consists rather in the fact that the old
contrast between blessing and curse is broken, and it is no longer
possible for God's people to be blessed and at the same time for
their enemies to be cursed. The exhortation "Bless those who
curse you" makes it possible for a Christian to live in such a way
that the blessing of his fellow humans no longer knows any
bounds. The church of Christ and the individual Christian no
longer need to curse anyone, because the work of Christ was on
behalf of their enemies as well.

(c) The commission of the apostles is related in Matthew
10:12–13 and Luke 10:5–6. In Matthew the structure of the commission is as follows:

Verse 1—Introduction. Jesus calls the twelve to him and gives
them power (1) to cast out unclean spirits; (2) to heal diseases
and infirmities.

Verses 2–4—The naming of the Twelve.

Verse 5a—The introduction is resumed, "charging them . . ."

Verses 5b–6—Instructions where to go.

Verses 7–8a—The twofold commission: (1) proclaim that the
kingdom of heaven is at hand; (2) heal the sick . . . cast out
demons.

Verses 8b–10—How to live: 8b, give without pay; 9, take no
money; 10a, take no equipment; 10b, the laborer deserves his
food.

Verses 11–15—Carrying out the commission: 11, inquiring
about a house; 12, greet those who receive you; 13, assurance of
the power of your greeting; 14, move on when no one welcomes
you; 15, punishment on such a house.

Verse 16—Concluding exhortation.

The term *bless* is not found in this parting speech, but it is certain that the greeting of a house in verse 12 is intended to be the greeting of blessing. The mere occurrence of such a blessing here, or the fact that Jesus told his disciples to give the greeting, is not in itself important. What is important is the function that this greeting of blessing has in the context of the commissioning of the apostles.

In Jesus' proclamation and work, blessing and greetings played no particular role. But when Jesus sends out his disciples something new is beginning. The message touches the existence of those who live at home, leading settled lives. The disciples are not commissioned to call people to leave their settled lives, as Jesus had called the disciples. It is not the disciples' task to call others to follow them but to proclaim in the cities, villages, and homes the message that the Kingdom is at hand. They themselves are told to continue their uncertain form of existence (vv. 8b–10), but they are not authorized to demand that those to whom they bring the message of the Kingdom enter on the wandering missionary life to which the disciples had been called by Jesus.

In this new situation in which the message of the apostles enters the settled lives of householders, blessing receives a new meaning. It is thus neither incidental nor accidental that a part of the apostles' commission is that they are to greet whatever home they enter.[66]

A similar transition in the Old Testament will help us understand what happened here. During the Exodus and the wandering in the wilderness, blessing played no role, and the terminology and the semantic domain of blessing are absent from the relevant texts. In the transition to the settled life, blessing takes on a specific meaning, as is seen in Deuteronomy in particular.

We are to consider the twofold commission of Jesus to his disciples in verses 7–8a in the same context (cf. Luke 10:9): "Preach as you go, saying, 'The kingdom of heaven is at hand.' Heal the sick, raise the dead, cleanse lepers, cast out demons." The disciples are sent out not only with the message of the coming of God's rule but also with the commission to heal and to help. Even if the healing of diseases and the driving out of demons are to be seen only as signs accompanying the message,

66. Cf. ibid., pp. 345–46.

the significance of the work of the disciples in helping and healing cannot be disputed, for it corresponds to the work of Jesus. This commission corresponds to the coming of the apostles into villages and homes as bearers of blessing in that the blessing and peace that were given and received in the exchange of greetings involves the same things that are involved in the mission of healing and helping—the well-being of the community and of men and women in community; their wholeness as creatures is also a part of this. The accounts in Acts show that this part of Jesus' commission was affirmed and followed by the apostles. They went about not only proclaiming a message but also helping, healing, and blessing.

In this way the task that Jesus committed to them corresponds exactly to the work of Jesus himself. That which the disciples received at no cost and passed on at no cost is the work of Jesus in these two aspects. Even if we were to interpret the work of Jesus as it is portrayed in the Gospels—healing, raising the dead, and driving out demons—by seeing it as related to the message of the coming of the Kingdom as signs of its coming, no one could still deny that the healings and exorcisms reveal a compassion for the suffering creation. This compassion (Matt. 9:36) is expressed again and again. Even if the writers of the Gospels regarded the message of Jesus' suffering, death, and resurrection as the central message that characterizes the gospel, they still all show how the path Jesus followed to his death and resurrection was marked by his compassion for the sufferings of his fellowmen and by the miracles that he performed for their material well-being.

The commissioning of the disciples in Matthew 10 begins with Jesus giving them the power to heal the sick and drive out demons, and also the charge to proclaim the gospel while performing these deeds. This shows conclusively that for this new situation in which the disciples no longer are calling people to follow Jesus in the narrow sense but are preaching to them as they remain settled in their homes and villages, this work of helping and healing, which is their work in relation to the concerns of this world, is a part of their commission. The greeting with which the disciples are sent out into the cities, villages, and homes has as its goal the same state of well-being that the commission to heal has.

Someone may object that the discourse in Matthew 10 and the parallels in Luke 9 and 10 form a skimpy textual basis for what has been said above. Granted. But this does make clear the reason the Gospels have so little to say about the work of Jesus and his disciples in bestowing blessing. Blessing first becomes significant where purely missionary work enters the stage of building communities that remain settled, and this work began with the sending out of the disciples. This indicates why it is in this context that blessing is spoken of repeatedly. In addition to the sending out of the disciples, we can find the same thing in Luke 24:50–51 or where Paul speaks of the fullness of the blessing of Christ which he hopes to bring to the church in Rome (Rom. 15:29).

Here a word may be said about the greetings at the beginning and end of the New Testament Epistles. We must remember that in investigating the meaning of blessing for the New Testament the greetings in the letters must be used with caution, since the possibility cannot be excluded that they represent a purely conventional form proper to letters. E. Lohmeyer advanced the thesis that the greetings of blessing in the New Testament letters had their original life setting in the worship of the early church.[67] G. Friedrich, however, attacked this view.[68] His critique drew on the work of Schenk, who wrote: "The greetings at the beginning and end of the New Testament letters are not specifically early Christian liturgical formulas of blessing, but are concrete intercessions with Christian content, put into epistolary form under the influence of the tradition of letter writing" (p. 92).

Peter Brunner, however, maintained the emphasis on the multiple connections of the epistolary greetings with the blessing in worship, pointing especially to the work of Gunther Bornkamm where he says, "At the conclusion of 1 Corinthians we find in 16:20–23 a series of liturgical formulas that were used in worship at the beginning of the celebration of the eucharist."[69] Brunner

67. "Probleme paulinischer Theologie," 1: "Briefliche Grussüberschriften" in *ZNW* 26 (1927) : 158ff.
68. "Lohmeyers These über das paulinische Briefpräskript kritisch betrachtet," *ThLZ* 81 (1956) : 343–46.
69. *Gesammelte Studien: Das Ende des Gesetzes, Paulusstudien* 1 (1952) : 123ff.; quoted in Brunner, "Der Segen," pp. 347–48.

concludes: "The Jewish greeting is without doubt a form of bless-ing. If we add to this our understanding of the greeting of peace that we find in the logion Luke 10:5-6 and Matthew 10:12-13, we are obliged to interpret the introductory greetings as effective words of blessing" (p. 348). I cannot here go into the dispute whether all or any of the formulas of greeting in the Epistles can be traced to the formulas of blessing or greeting. Even if there were no connection at all, as seems probable from the present state of the discussion, the question whether the epistolary greet-ings are derived from formulas used in worship is not decisive. The only important thing is that the greetings in the Epistles as such, quite independent of their wording, characterize a new situation in contrast to the proclamation and ministry of Jesus. The apostles are now dealing with congregations that are settled in specific places and therefore lead a different existence from that of the apostles and that of Jesus. For the dealings of the apostles with these settled communities, and this holds also for letters to individuals, who, after all, were members of such com-munities, greetings assume a special, essential meaning because they are a part of arrival and departure. This means that there is a correspondence between the instruction to give a greeting in Matthew 10 and the greetings at the beginning and end of the letters of the New Testament, as Brunner correctly saw.

It is true, as G. Friedrich and others have pointed out, that the vocabulary of the greetings in letters is not specifically Christian but was borrowed from both Jewish and non-Jewish traditions. That does not alter the fact that this vocabulary belongs to the semantic domain of blessing (blessing, peace, presence with, etc.) and that the greetings show how blessing came to have meaning for the settled communities. I want to point out in passing that this conclusion gives us a new point of view from which to look at the question of worship in the early church. The gathering of a congregation in a purely missionary situation is and must be something different from what we customarily call worship. And since in the New Testament, including the letters, a missionary situation is present to a large degree, it is useless to attempt to demonstrate the nature of Christian worship directly from the New Testament or to derive it from the New Testament. We must rather begin with the assumption that Christian worship in the real sense arose out of the transition from the missionary situation to the life of the settled community, and that therefore the structure of Christian worship contains elements of a settled nature that are not a part of the gathering of a community in a purely missionary situation. One of these elements characteristic of settled life is the bestowal of blessing at the conclusion of worship and the giving of a greeting at its beginning.

Summary

What have we learned about the use and the meaning of the concept of blessing in the New Testament?

The word is found in three types of situations: God blesses, Christ blesses, and men bless. The majority of the passages are of the first type. Only a few passages report that Christ or a man blesses. The question then of whether the greetings in the Epistles belong here can remain open. It is now possible to arrange the passages according to content, and no longer according to form, as we did at the beginning of this section.

(a) In a number of passages blessing is mentioned or described as an occurrence in the Old Covenant, without establishing any connection to Christ or to the saving events of the New Covenant. This would include from group 3 (Schenk's group I) Hebrews 6:14 and 12:17 and from group 5 (III) Hebrews 11:20, 21 and 7:1–7. Passages of this type are found only in Hebrews.

But in other passages blessing is often presupposed as having taken place in the Old Covenant or is specifically mentioned in quotations, especially of Genesis 12:1–3.

Not a single New Testament passage that mentions blessing in the Old Covenant or gives a quotation about blessing or uses it as an example speaks in a derogatory way of blessing as found in the Old Testament. It is never presented as being in competition with or in contrast to the events of salvation in the New Testament or their benefits.

(b) A deliberate and pronounced transformation of the concept of blessing in the sense of a Christianization or a modification through the activities of Christ can be found in three types of contexts.

(1) In Galatians 3:8–9, Acts 3:25–26, and Ephesians 1:3 the Old Testament concept of blessing is basically altered. Here blessing means the saving acts of God in Christ, or the justification that is effected in these acts. The concept of blessing has a Christological or soteriological meaning. Galatians 3 and Acts 3 establish a relationship to Genesis 12:1–3, the passage in the Old Testament that most clearly indicates the incorporation of the previously unhistorical concept of blessing into the history of God's activity with his people.

(2) In Romans 15:29 the new expression "blessing of Christ" indicates a new use of the concept of blessing in the Christian community. Blessing is spoken of in reference to the fact that proclamation of the gospel brings about the growth, prosperity, and strengthening of the community. This is a new formulation that does not identify blessing with God's saving work in Christ or with justification, as in (1) above, but describes the work of Christ in terms of its effects and, in doing so, incorporates an element that originally belonged to the concept of blessing.

(3) The third change can be seen in the passages of group III, with its exhortation to bless those who curse you (Luke 6:28; Rom. 12:14; 1 Cor. 4:12; 1 Pet. 3:9). The Christianization here consists in the breaking of the old contrast between blessing and curse. This exhortation enables the Christian to lead an existence in which the blessing on our fellowman no longer has a limit formed by the cursing of our enemies.

(c) The concept of blessing is used in a number of passages in which the future consummation of salvation is described. This occurs in Matthew 25:34 ("O blessed of my Father") and in the passages that speak of "inheriting blessing" (1 Pet. 3:7; Heb. 6:7–8; 6:12, 14; 12:17). Here too we can speak of a Christianization of blessing, but the basic Old Testament concept in the same type of context (Isa. 65:23–24) is not essentially altered.

(d) In all passages where Jesus is the one who blesses, the concept of blessing is that of the Old Testament and the Jewish community, and each time there is a traditional occasion for blessing: the blessing of the children (Mark 10:13–16), blessing the bread (Luke 9:16; 22:17; 24:30 and parallels), and the blessing at parting (Luke 24:50–51). The specific feature of the occurrence in each instance is that the one blessing is the savior, or the Christ. In each case the blessing is subordinated to a saving act of Christ but not absorbed into it.

When the disciples are commissioned (Matt. 10; Luke 10), they are sent out not merely with the message of the coming of the kingdom but also with the powerful greeting of blessing, and this corresponds to the twofold division of the mission as preaching and healing. Blessing takes on meaning wherever the message touches the existence of those who are settled in their houses, villages, and cities. The greetings of blessing in New Testament letters belong in the same context.

Therefore we can say by way of conclusion the following:

The New Testament presents a basic transformation in which blessing is displaced by God's saving act in Christ and by justification. But alongside this, in a way that corresponds to the historicizing of the concept by the Yahwist, the concept of blessing that came down from the Old Testament retained its meaning:

• in the blessings bestowed by Jesus, which unite the procedures of blessing and their interpretation from the Old Testament with the specific work of Jesus;

• in the blessings bestowed by the disciples, which was a part of their commission, along with proclamation;

• in the "blessing of Christ," which is effective in strengthening the churches and making them grow;

• in the description of the consummation of salvation as "the inheriting of blessing."

To present a comprehensive picture of the continuing significance of the Old Testament concept of blessing for the New Testament, it is not enough to look only at the usage of the terms *eulogein* and *eulogia*. In addition, we must consider the semantic domain of blessing and the terminology of the areas mentioned above:

• The presence of the exalted Lord with his community, his remaining with them.

• The element of continuity in the life of the congregations—growth, maturation, strengthening, and so on.

• The corresponding element of continuity in the life of the individual.

• The language that stresses our nature as creatures, in the continuity of the life of the community and of the individual.
• The description of the consummation of salvation, in which deliverance and the history of deliverance come to their conclusion.

CHAPTER 3

Blessing in Worship and in

the Rituals of the Church

THE MEANING AND FUNCTION OF
BLESSING IN WORSHIP

Its Basis in the History of Blessing

The presupposition of the following section is that the function and significance of blessing in worship and in the rituals of the church—whether of a practical, liturgical nature or a systematic, doctrinal nature—must stand in a recognizable relation to what the Bible says about God's blessing and about blessing as an institution.[1]

This does not mean that blessing in the rites of the church in our day should be a direct continuation or an imitation of a ritual of blessing that we might find somewhere in the Bible. It does mean, however, that the bestowal of blessing in today's church is a responsible practice only if it is based on a comprehensive knowledge of the biblical data. Even if we were to reject what the Bible says about blessing as without meaning for the church, that rejection would require this comprehensive knowledge as its precondition.

For such a comprehensive view, it must be noted that what the New Testament says about blessing is in every instance related to and derived from what the Old Testament says. What blessing means can be determined only on the basis of the whole Bible and not from the New Testament alone.

It must also be noted that both Testaments speak of blessing in two ways. First there is the activity or rite of blessing, espe-

1. On the history of blessing in Christian worship, see K. Frör, in *Leiturgia* 2 (1954) : 588–92.

cially the blessing of a group or an individual by a priest during worship. But the Bible also speaks of a blessing of God that is in no way bound to a form or an act. In it God, as the one who blesses, is independent of any institution, acting when and where he chooses.

These two possibilities of speaking about blessing point to a history of blessing in the Bible. This history provides the basis for our investigation of blessing in the present-day practice of the church. Aware of it or not, the church today, with its understanding of blessing and its rites, stands in a history of blessing regardless of whether or not it wants to be a part of that history.

The history of blessing in the Bible underwent two great transformations that were of basic significance for our understanding of blessing and our manner of bestowing it. The first was the uniting of blessing with history by the Yahwist. In this transformation it became impossible to regard blessing any longer as a magical act or a magical transfer of power. The linguistic expression of this transformation is the wish, which corresponds to the connection of blessing with promise. In this linguistic form the conviction is expressed that in the blessing of the community by a man or by a priest, it is God who really bestows the blessing, as the basic passage (Num. 6) shows explicitly. It is God's blessing that is imparted to the members of the community who leave one another to return to their homes and their work. That it is God's blessing means that this blessing is intended to convey what both the Old and the New Testaments say about God's blessing.

The second great transformation in the history of blessing is the combination of blessing with the work of Christ. When blessing is imparted in a service of Christian worship, at the center of which is the message of God's saving deeds in Christ, this means that blessing can be understood, imparted, and received only in terms of the transformation which the concept underwent in God's work in Christ.

The decisive factor is that through God's work in Christ death is no longer a limit to God's bestowal of blessing. As a consequence, cursing of others is abolished as a limit to and a necessary supplement to the bestowal of blessing by believers. In this way, cursing in every form, even a spiritualized form, is eliminated from Christian worship. Where such cursing still occurred in worship in the history of the church, it was based on a failure to recognize the transformation that took place when blessing became united to the work of Christ.

As a result of the death and resurrection of Jesus Christ, death is no longer the limit of God's work of blessing, and consequently blessing shares in the hidden nature of God's work in the cross of Christ. Blessing can no longer automatically be recognized in what occurs but may be hidden in the cross and in death. A part of the acceptance of God's blessing in the name of Jesus Christ is the acceptance and affirmation of the way God's work of blessing is hidden.

This transformation of blessing through God's work in Christ can find its expression in the use of the sign of the cross as a sign of bestowing blessing, but this is not essential.

CONCLUDING BLESSING AND OPENING GREETING

The origin of the blessing that concludes worship is the greeting at parting. The final greeting and the blessing of the one or ones departing were originally one and the same. When we recall this origin of the blessing bestowed as the congregation is dismissed from worship, we see that it is not basically a sacral act. It is a procedure that normally occurs when people have gathered and then take leave of one another before each goes his own way. Even the fact that this blessing is bestowed in the name of God does not introduce an absolute distinction between it and a parting greeting outside of worship. Every greeting was once a greeting in the name of God.

The distinctive feature of the concluding blessing in worship is found in the nature of the activities that it concludes. A cultic event, a service of worship, a feast, or a festival that is concluded with a blessing are distinguished by being "sacred events," however that may be understood. It is not essential that emphasis be placed on a holy place ("We bless you from the house of the Lord," Ps. 118:26) or on a holy time, as in blessing at a high festival, or on the particular holiness of the one imparting the blessing or even on the holy procedure itself. It is not even decisive whether the sacred event is seen as depending more on the sacramental elements in it or on the word proclaimed to the congregation. The sole decisive feature for the nature of the concluding blessing is that the service of worship, that is, that for which the community came together, has this nature of a holy, distinctive event. It is an event in which God and his community that has gathered for worship participate together and reciprocally. The distinctive feature of the holiness of what occurs there results from the fact that it is God who speaks and acts in these events and that those who have gathered there respond to him. This alone makes the parting blessing something special. The blessing is a bridge that joins what happens in worship to what takes place outside. What has happened there is imparted to those who now leave one another to return to their daily lives. However worship may be organized or interpreted, every type of worship determines the relationship between what happens in worship and what happens outside, and it is in this relationship that the blessing at the conclusion of worship has its function. Here the ecumenical significance of blessing is seen. Whether worship has a highly sacramental form or is a completely de-sacralized, simple gathering called just "a gathering" (*qahal*, "gathering," is a designation for worship in the Old Testament), that relationship is something all forms of worship share, and it therefore is the place where blessing functions.

The opening greeting at the beginning of worship corresponds to the blessing at its close with which the community is dismissed. It is also important to bring to bear here what the Bible shows us about greetings and the relationship of blessing to greeting. First of all, it is clear that opening greeting and concluding blessing belong together, just as do everyday greetings and leave-taking. Here it becomes clear why the parting blessing is unilateral and the initial greeting mutual. This corresponds to the ancient forms of greeting in the Old Testament. When people meet they greet each other, but when they part the one who is going away receives a blessing. When the initial greeting by the leader of worship, "The Lord be with you," is answered by the congregation, this exchange of greetings expresses the fact that this is the introduction to an encounter between the congregation that has gathered for worship and the God who acts and speaks in worship, the Lord of the community. The function of the opening greeting in worship can have meaning only when the congregation understands it as a real greeting and speaks (or sings) it as such. A part of this meaning is expressed when the congregation recognizes the simple meaning of the words of greeting, "The Lord be with you," as essentially a blessing in one of the forms of the language of blessing. In the Old Testament, saying that God is present can be another expression for God's blessing. The purpose of the greeting is to make those who are greeted aware that through worship God will be present with them. The response, "And with you," is directed to the one who is authorized to conduct this service of worship, the one who speaks God's word to us and distributes to us the bread and wine of the Lord's Supper. If this greeting is taken seriously, there is no need for a special prayer before the sermon, customary in many places, for the success of the service or for God's blessing on his word. This is the purpose of the greeting at the start of worship. Much depends then on understanding and taking seriously both the blessing and the greeting in their simplest meaning as parts of the total service of worship. We need also to rethink the repetition of the "salutation" in a service of worship, as is provided for in many liturgies. Such repetition of the greeting would obscure or spoil its true function as greeting.

The greeting as the congregation gather and the final blessing as they go their way have an additional significance for our worship services. They are physical functions and they make it clear that our whole being as men and women is involved in worship. Just as every ordinary meeting begins with a greeting and ends with taking leave of each other, so worship is cast in the ordinary human mold of greeting and leave-taking. It is precisely the human side of the meeting of the community for worship that is emphasized in greeting and blessing. In the present day we are more and more inclined to regard worship as a purely spiritual procedure and to experience it as such. The more we regard the sermon as the essential part and everything else as the formal setting for the sermon, the more we lose the biblical insight that wherever God speaks he addresses us in our total being. But there is no mistaking the fact that the greeting and the blessing involve the total person, body, soul, and spirit. And because greeting and blessing are directed to our bodily existence, the proper gesture is a vital part. The gesture that accompanies the blessing does not represent a sacral or magical meaning that some think lies behind it, but rather it expresses the truth that the entire person receives the blessing.

The origin of the blessing in leave-taking and the corresponding origin of the greeting at the beginning of worship in the greeting in everyday life makes it clear that these two elements are not so different from each other as a long liturgical tradition might make it seem. What was said above about the relationship between the two can once again become reality for us. The greeting in worship and that in everyday life can have a reciprocal relationship. The secular greeting that has become a mere formality can take on new vitality from what happens in worship, and the greeting in worship can be rediscovered as a real greeting, in which the situation plays a role. The significance of this mutual relationship can preserve for the greeting and blessing in worship the nature of real greetings, and it can preserve the greetings of daily life from drying up, by giving them new liveliness and warmth, so that the one whom we greet is affirmed as our fellow creature.

The Christian church should ponder the significance of the fact that in greeting and blessing something not specifically Christian has been taken into its worship, something that is common to all humanity and has a good and necessary role to play in our worship.

THE MEANING OF BLESSING FOR THE WHOLE OF WORSHIP

Worship is often interpreted in terms of God's saving actions in Christ in the same one-dimensional way that salvation is interpreted in theological thought.

In this view the only decisive occurrence in worship is the proclamation of the message of God's saving work in Christ and the congregation's response to that message. To be sure, this is the center of Protestant worship, but it is not the whole of worship. Worship mediates not only God's saving activity but his bless-

ing as well. Therefore greeting and blessing are unconditionally a part of worship, as the Reformers believed they should be.[2]

> Brunner says: "The greeting includes a blessing, the characteristic
> feature of which is its place at the beginning of the ritual. The
> blessing in the specific sense comes at the end. It is pronounced at
> the point of departure. . . . The structure of the formulas of greet-
> ing and blessing has in common with the formula of absolution
> that it is a performative word. . . . In the blessing, as in absolution,
> the sacramental character of the word is particularly clear. . . .
> Greeting and blessing are among the most important things that
> occur in worship."[3]

But it is not only the greeting at the start of worship and the
benediction at its end that mediate God's blessing. There is also
emphasis on the continuous activity of God, which is a necessary
part of worship as we know it and which corresponds to the continuous work of God in his blessings to his people.

The regular rhythm from Sunday to Sunday and from year to
year corresponds to the rhythm of God's continued work (Gen.
8:22). The message of God's saving work in Christ does not as
such demand this rhythm. There is no New Testament basis for
saying that every Sunday we must proclaim the message of what
God has done for us in Christ. Nor is there any basis in the New
Testament for the cyclical celebration through the year of the
events that were determinative in the life of Christ—nativity,
death, resurrection, ascension, bestowal of the Spirit. Both the
rhythm of the week and the rhythm of the annual festivals were
there before the message of Christ. The form of proclamation
that we find in the New Testament is that of the missionary
sermon, but such a sermon depends on the specific situation and
cannot be tied to a cyclical rhythm. Such a rhythm is possible
only in a settled life with its resulting orderliness. The order that
makes the rhythm of years and weeks possible is the result of
God's orderly work, his bestowal of blessing and peace.

This means that the combining of the message of God's saving

---

2. On the meaning of blessing in worship, see Brunner, *Leiturgia* 1 (1954):
200–203.
3. Ibid.

deeds in Christ with the rhythm of weekly worship and of annual celebrations of God's works corresponds to the combining of salvation and blessing. We must not lose sight of the fact that the rhythm of our worship does not have its origin in the Christ events; it is based on God's bestowal of blessing rather than on his saving deeds. And we must be aware that a long-term separation of this rhythm from proclamation would mean the end of worship.

But it is not only the constant rhythm of weeks and years that is based on God's blessing but also the constant nature of the language used in worship. Sacral or liturgical language is not merely language bound by tradition. It is fixed and unchanging because it presents anew God's constant activity in words that correspond to that constancy. It was thus a basic error to justify liturgically fixed language, the typical language of worship, by saying that it is the form which corresponds to the proclamation of the gospel and is appropriate to that proclamation. It has nothing to do with proclamation as such. All the elements of this sacral language were there long before the coming of Christ, and they grew out of pre-Christian traditions of worship. Proclamation of the gospel as such is not tied in any way to a sacral language shared by cultic practices. Such language comes into play where worship takes on the nature of something abiding, and the bestowal of blessing is added to the proclamation of the gospel.

When we recognize that worship is concerned both with God's work of salvation and his work in blessing, and that the blessing bestowed in the name of the God who blesses is an essential part of the proclamation of the message of Christ and the congregation's response to it, then we have an adequate basis for our present-day questions about the form and language of worship and about the relevance of what occurs in worship. This leads us to a necessary and helpful clarification. Any attempt to reformulate worship along only one of these two lines must be abandoned. It is not possible to formulate an order of worship or a language of worship merely on the basis of a liturgical tradition, using elements of a liturgical schema divorced from proclamation in the midst of the world. But neither is it possible to base the form and language of worship solely on the proclamation of God's saving deeds in Christ. That would be possible in a purely missionary sermon, but not for ongoing worship in a settled situation.

From the outset the basic structure of Christian worship must be seen as polar in nature. Since it is concerned with communicating God's work of salvation as well as his blessing, it must contain an equal emphasis on the missionary element and on the liturgical element. The proclamation of the message demands a language that is understood by our contemporaries and that corresponds to the current situation, and is thus constantly changing. In contrast, blessing demands a form of worship and a language that remain the same, united vertically with the successive generations and horizontally with the whole Christian world. It is by no means impossible to combine in one service of worship these two seemingly contradictory elements. When we recognize that both basic elements, the constant and the variable, belong together, and that only when both are present do we have a truly living worship, then a wide range of possibilities opens up.

When we recognize that the essence of worship involves both a constant and a variable element, we will be more cautious about expressing absolute judgments and making absolute decisions. We will be cautious about claiming that a specific form of worship is the only correct form and all others are false. We will also be more cautious with experimentation. What is constant will be found in the polarity of the basic structure that determines the essence of Christian worship, a structure that contains the possibility of many developments.

A recognition of this polar structure can also advance ecumenical discussion of worship. If we can be united in this, it will be much easier to recognize and describe the things we have in common in the different traditions.

GOD'S BLESSING IN THE HYMNS OF THE CHURCH

The church's hymns show more clearly than anything else that the church has always been aware of God's bestowal of blessing

in addition to the salvation he gives through Christ. All hymnals
contain songs that have nothing at all to say of God's work of
salvation in Christ, that is, they are not Christological or soteriological but sing only of the blessings God bestows. There are, first
of all, hymns that correspond to the descriptive praise of the
Psalter, such as "Praise to the Lord, the Almighty."[4] And there
are others that celebrate the coming of morning and evening,
such as "Evening and Morning."[5] There are also hymns that
mark the passing of the year and celebrate the new year. In many
others God's work of saving and his work of blessing are combined, for instance, "Bless, O My Soul, the Living God,"[6] which
is based on Psalm 103.

Hymns related to the festivals commemorating the events in
Christ's life are based solely on God's saving activity and correspond to the psalms of declarative praise in the Psalter. It is
interesting to note that among the Christmas hymns, in addition
to the older ones that are completely dominated by the theme of
God's work in sending his Son to save the world, or of the in-
carnation, there are hymns in which almost unnoticed the theme
of blessing takes the place of salvation. An especially clear example is "Each Year the Christ Child Comes Again. . . ."[7]

The hymns that express in song the congregation's response
should bring clearly to our awareness the polarity of God's saving work and his bestowal of blessing. Our service of worship
should express clearly the way in which our praise of what God
has done is to encompass everything, from the central act of salvation to the furthest limits of God's blessing. In this way it will
correspond to our intercessions, which have the same center and
the same limits.[8]

4. "Lobe den Herren, den mächtigen . . ."
5. "Die güldne Sonne . . ."
6. "Nun lob' mein' Seel' den Herren . . ."
7. "Alle Jahre wieder kommt das Christuskind . . ."
8. The divisions of the *Evangelisches Kirchengesangbuch,* the hymnbook of
the Evangelical Church in Germany, are in part quite nonsensical, and they
should provide an occasion for us to examine the hymns anew in terms of
their basic structure, following as a pattern the categories of the psalms of
the Old Testament.

THE MEANING OF BLESSING IN THE
RITES OF THE CHURCH

BLESSING AT BAPTISM AND THE LORD'S SUPPER

In many of the rites of the church, blessing is important simply because it occupies a central position in the liturgy. We need to think through its meaning and function on the basis of the principles worked out in the preceding pages. There is room here for only a few suggestions.

(a) *Blessing at baptism.* We must first of all make it clear that blessing is not identical with baptism, nor is it a meaningless appendage to it. The important thing is to differentiate clearly between the act of baptism and the bestowal of blessing. The incorporation of a new member into the community by baptism has in itself nothing to do with the blessing and could take place without it. The addition of the blessing to the act of the baptism of a child means that the one baptized is brought not only under the authority of the God who saves but also into the realm ruled by the God who blesses. The possible misunderstanding of baptism can be avoided only if a clear distinction is made between the two rites and the blessing at baptism is given once again its proper meaning.

The question of infant baptism could be clarified if a distinction were made between baptism and blessing. The story of Jesus blessing the children, which is often read at baptism, cannot serve as a basis for baptism but it can for the blessing of a child. It is the appropriate text for the bestowal of such a blessing. None of the objections that are raised today against the baptism of infants or children can be applied to the bestowal of blessing on them. Any effort toward a new form of baptism must be based on the fundamental distinction between baptism and blessing.

(b) *Blessing during the observance of the Lord's Supper.* The inclusion of blessing in the accounts of the celebration of the Lord's Supper in the Gospels and in Paul's account ("The cup of blessing which we bless . . ." 1 Cor. 10:16) shows that from the beginning the celebration of the Lord's Supper included God's work in bestowing blessing. The way was prepared for this by the custom of blessing the food at a meal, a custom that Jesus adopted. This blessing includes the giving of thanks for the nourishment of food. The blessing of a meal has two functions. It binds those who eat into a community in the sight of God, and it offers the praise and thanksgiving of the community to God.

The blessing of the bread and wine has its own distinctive meaning in addition to its role in consecrating these elements in their relationship to the body and blood of Christ. In no case should the blessing be understood as a consecration or transformation of the elements. Both procedures are to be distinguished —the consecration, however it is interpreted, and the blessing. The consecration involves the work of the God who saves and it makes present to us through the words of the Supper the suffering and death of Christ. The blessing is concerned with God's work of making grain grow and ripen and his work of creating and preserving the community of those who take part in the meal.

The blessing at the Lord's Supper has then the same meaning that the disciples found in their being together for the Last Supper with their Lord and for the meals that they shared as they traveled about with him. That last meal formed the link between the meals at which Jesus had spoken the blessing during their journeys and the celebrations that would make his work present to them again after his departure. He remained with them not only as the Savior but also as the Lord who blesses.

Blessing in the Official Rites of the Church

The bestowal of blessing as a part of the rites of the church that mark the stages of life must be seen as a procedure that stands on its own. In the decades since the industrialization and secularization of society, the so-called official rites of the church have become an increasing problem, which has a sociological as well as a theological side. Here I will deal only with its theological aspects. In these rites, blessing takes on considerable importance because it constitutes an important part of the rites and they cannot be thought of without it. There is therefore no way to avoid reflecting anew on the meaning and function of blessing as a part of these rites.

It has long been considered good form in Protestant churches to disparage the bestowal of blessing at the transition points of life. Attention is called to the misunderstanding of blessing as something magical, and blessing is belittled as a sort of religious life insurance. It is pointed out that a blessing at such important occasions has nothing specifically Christian about it. The issue is dismissed by saying that those who desire a blessing or who ask for the church's blessing are not thinking of God the Father of Jesus Christ. They are not thinking, it is claimed, of the gospel, but only of the blessing. This "only" is a constant refrain in whatever is said about blessing in the context of the rites of the church. Blessing is assumed to be something of a lesser nature, less valuable, inauthentic. Corresponding to this deprecating way of speaking about blessing is the pathos with which it is stressed that the authentic element in all such rites—baptism, confirmation, marriage, burial, anniversaries, and similar occasions—is the proclamation of the gospel.

We must clarify our understanding of what the church is doing in these rites. Clarity will come only when we recognize the alternatives that we confront. On the one hand we could hold the opinion that the only task of the church is the proclamation of the message of salvation in Christ. Then the church would have to have a form that would direct all its powers solely to the accomplishment of this task. Such rites as weddings and funerals would then not be an essential part of its work. It is not possible in one breath to belittle blessing as inauthentic and in the next breath to urge the pastor of an urban congregation to devote a major part of his time and energy to performing such official duties. It is often said today that this issue involves the nature of the "national church," and this is not something that should be abandoned lightly or without appreciation of what it has meant; to say this involves a dangerous shift of the problem. It is a question not of the form of the church but of its task. Only when the so-called official rites are based on the commission given by the Lord of the church can they be carried out in obedience to him.

Historical considerations might indicate that we ought to give up the administration of these rites and concentrate all the church's powers on the proclamation of the gospel. The rites of the church at significant transitions in life must be seen in terms of the history of religion as being closely related to the so-called rites of passage, that is, sacral ceremonies that protect and preserve our existence at dangerous transitions such as birth, puberty, marriage, and death.[9] These rites go back to the earliest stages of religion and are found in clearly developed form in primitive religions. It is impossible to deny that there is a connection between the observances in the rites of the church and rites of passage in pre-Christian and non-Christian societies. Confirmation, for example, still has a close relationship to puberty ceremonies and initiations among primitive peoples. If the only task of the church were the proclamation of the message of Christ, there would be no need for a rite that bestows a blessing at the transition to puberty. Then if the state claimed a monopoly of such rites the church could easily turn them over to it and stop performing them. The church can hold fast to confirmation and struggle to preserve it only if it has a clear connection to the task set by the Lord of the church.

If it is asked how such rites at the crucial transitions of life came to be practiced in the church, the answer is obvious. It happened when the church entered into a settled life, even though this cannot be demonstrated in every instance. In any case this is the reason that the New Testament does not speak of such rites and that no direct New Testament basis can be found for them. A church devoted totally to its missionary task cannot be interested in funeral rituals. More appropriate is the saying "Leave the dead to bury their own dead; but as for you, go and proclaim the kingdom of God" (Luke 9:60). The extensive transformation that resulted from the change to a settled life has a parallel in the Old Testament, where the settling of the Israelite tribes in the land led to extensive changes in worship. (For details, see

9. See Arnold van Gennep, *Les Rites de Passage* (Paris, 1909), and the various texts in the history of religion.

what I said in the earlier parts of this book about the history of blessing in the Old Testament.)

If, however, the church's rites dealing with the crises of life constitute a task that cannot be abandoned because they are based on the command of the Lord of the church, their justification is to be found in the blessing that was a part of the work of Jesus Christ himself and that was expressed also in his commission to the disciples when he sent them out into the world (Matt. 10). But this must be also seen in the larger context of what the entire Bible says about blessing. Blessing is concerned with people throughout their lives, with their birth and maturity, with the union of man and woman and the birth of children, with aging and death. The message of the gospel encounters a person somewhere in his or her life, and then it is not only the before and after that are important, as shown in Romans 7; God's bestowal of blessing is concerned with the whole of human life. It is for this reason that the blessing which accompanies a person throughout life and is bestowed at certain points in the special rites of the church finds its necessary significance.

This significance of the rites of the church must also have an effect on the proclamation that takes place at the center of the church's life, the proclamation of God's saving deeds in Christ on our behalf. I will illustrate this at only one point. It is impossible for a Christocentric, strictly soteriological sermon to speak to anyone except human beings in general. It is the human person in general who is lost without Christ and who is redeemed by the death of Jesus on the cross. When this is proclaimed it is immaterial whether the hearer is man or woman, whether he or she is twenty, fifty, or eighty years old, pupil or teacher, or climbing the ladder of life or descending it. Anyone who year after year has preached sermons or listened to them knows how hard it is for anyone to feel that he or she is addressed as an individual who is at a particular point in life, if the sermon is couched in such general terms. Every preacher is familiar with this problem. The preacher can deal with it better if he regularly turns to his sermon preparation from the performance of his official rites, in which he was not dealing with people in general but with infants or boys and girls or husbands and wives or with elderly people at the point of death. This side of his task will again and again make it clear to him that his proclamation of God's saving work in Christ cannot be separated from his work in bestowing blessing. There are no people in general; there are always only specific people in their communities and at specific points in the ascending or descending course of life.

This relationship of specific church rites to specific stages of life must be recognized if the relationship of each of these rites to the message of salvation in Christ is to be seen in its full meaning and its relevance. Each of these rites has then a relationship both to the message of Christ and to God's blessing.

On this basis it is possible to see also the indirect missionary meaning of the rites of the church. This would be missed if in performing a wedding the pastor disregarded the specific task that is expected of him, that is, to speak a word that is relevant to this unique hour in the life of this particular couple and their families. If he uses the wedding as the occasion for preaching a sermon that proclaims only what is Christian in general, relevant to everyone at any time, he is failing to use his missionary opportunity. Only if he takes seriously the situation of the group to whom he speaks through the rite in its specific nature and unique time and then speaks to that situation, so that everyone taking part, whether it is a baptism, a wedding, or a funeral, can see that this unique situation is being taken seriously, only then can he fulfill his missionary purpose. This can take place because what is said about God's blessing is taken seriously as applicable to the specific situation.

When the full meaning of blessing in the rite is recognized, it comes about naturally that the sermon or meditation speaks to the specific, unique hour of the group that is gathered, so that they hear the word that has been prepared with them in mind and spoken directly to them. The friend of the groom who is there with the other guests may have no relation at all to the church, but he can still see from the wedding sermon that the pastor is truly concerned about this couple and their affirmation of each other and that he has something he truly wants to share with them.

The nature of the message addressed to the hearers will be determined by the pastor's understanding of blessing. Blessing is intended for a person at a specific point on the trajectory from birth to death. That this blessing is imparted to the Christian community in the name of Christ and is therefore a Christian blessing can be seen in the way in which the specific situation of those assembled is brought into relationship with the work of Jesus Christ and with his church.

In conclusion, something should be said in reference to the alleged misunderstanding of the rites as magic, a question that often comes up in discussions about the rites of the church. We must keep in mind that blessing has its history prior to the rise of Christianity and outside of Christianity. A purely Christian blessing, that is, a blessing that arose *de novo* on the basis of the Christ event, does not exist. Blessing was a part of the inheritance that Jesus and his community and the entire New Testament received from the past. Blessing has a prehistory that reaches beyond the Old Testament and the Semitic high religions back into primitive religions. The bestowal of blessing was once a magical rite, but this magical quality was first eliminated in the Old Testament not in the New. It occurred through the way in which God's promise was combined with the history of God's people.

Today we too can best avoid the possible misunderstanding of the bestowal of blessing as magic by seeing blessing in the rites of the church as a part of the history of God's work with his people, the history of the course of Christianity in our time and our world toward that goal where Christ waits for us.

The radical secularizing of our whole existence proceeds so rapidly today that the misunderstanding of a rite such as the blessing of a child at baptism as magic will soon cease to be a problem. There will no longer be any need for such a psuedo-sacral reassurance. Instead, we can expect in increasing measure that the meaning blessing has for the community of those who ask for it will become clearer and more important.

In the Old Testament, blessing had its origin in the family and was related to the forms of family life as community. Since the groups that gather for such church rites as baptism, confirmation, marriage, and burial are basically family groups, the blessing the church bestows in these rites is especially directed toward life within the family. In a time when we are moving into a mass society, this relationship of blessing to the family takes on increased significance. These rites constitute today a particular opportunity for the church, since the blessing imparted in them involves the well-being and peace of family life. For this reason if no other, it would be irresponsible in our present situation to belittle or abandon these rites.

As the church confronts the tasks and possibilities awaiting it here, it should remind itself of the positive significance of blessing, especially in those rites that deal with the stages of life. We will then be able to expect that those who desire the blessing of the church for their new baby, for their marriage, for a new stage of life, truly desire the blessing of the church of Jesus Christ, at the center of which is the message of his cross and resurrection. Then the blessing bestowed in the name of Christ will really reach into the life and activities of the family. If blessing is taken seriously in the rites of the church in their specific function for the limited community of the family, the possibility arises that we can once again establish a firm connection between these rites that deal with the stages of life and the heart of the church's proclamation.

Indexes

NAMES AND SUBJECTS

SCRIPTURE REFERENCES